Ask Yourself This...
The Easy Way to Write Your Life Story

by

David Eubanks

PROPERTY OF
BERWICK
ROYAL OAK
LIBRARY

Ask Yourself This... Copyright © 2003 by David Eubanks. All rights reserved. Printed in the United States of America. No part of this book may be used or reproduced in any manner whatsoever without written permission except in the case of brief quotations embodied in critical articles and reviews. For information write David Eubanks, 29W451 Emerald Green Drive, Warrenville, Illinois 60555.

Table of Contents

Why Write a Personal Biography? 1
Will Anybody Read It? 11
Before You Write 13
Modes of Development 15
Organizing the Information 19
The Big Secret to Telling Your Story 25
    Starting Anywhere, Going Anywhere 36
    Indexing 37
What If I Can't Remember? 39
The Difference Is in the Details 43
Telling What Happened 47
    Choices, Changes, Gains and Losses 53
Emotional Integrity 59
Show and Tell 65
    Close Your Eyes And Type 65
Questioning Exercises 71
    What can you question? 71
Design And Layout 89
    How to Create a Master Folder 107
    Compiling the Files into One File 110
    Including Photographs 112
    Pagination 119
    Scanning and Photoediting 122
Transcribing Techniques 125
Quick Reference 127
Some Reflective Questions 129
Topics to Ask Yourself About 131
The Whole You 133

Why Write a Personal Biography?

"The only normal people are the ones you don't know very well."

- Joe Ancis

If your great grandfather had written a book about himself, would you want to read it?

Of course, you would. There isn't a life story on earth not worth telling. If you're thinking that your life is too boring (or too "normal") to be worth reading, I encourage the suspension of that belief. Every life told with ample detail will be interesting to the family. No one's life is a cookie cutter copy of another's. It is always interesting to read how another has handled any one of life's commonplace challenges. Or the ordeals. Or the victories. Or anything.

Every autobiography, memoir or oral history is an automatic best seller in the family.

Consider the circumstance of finding a pack of letters in an attic trunk of an abandoned house. The letters are wrapped in a ribbon. You sit in the stagnant air of the dimly lit space holding the letters. Who among us would not be tempted to open one then and there and read it? We want to know what's in them. Even a stranger's letters hold an irresistible appeal.

Go ahead, do this. Write your story.

You've picked up this text with the idea of recording your life somehow. I encourage you to stay the course, whether

Why Write a Personal Biography?

you write this text yourself or employ someone else to help. What you are about to do is not for you. It's for the family. It is not about vanity. It's an act of generosity.

We live in a time when there has been a displacement of family continuity and values by a stream of media-produced vulgarity. Movies and television depict family and personal relationship in shallow scenes of mutual disrespect. They have cheapened the value of our humanity as though family itself doesn't matter anymore.

Today's children may know more of any pop artist's personal history than their own grandparents, and perhaps, their parents too. Something essential is missing. For that matter, something has always been missing in the linkage of ancestors to posterity.

Historians and archeologists search high and low for a soldier's letter to salvage, or a shard of some broken tool to dig up, or to see some primitively carved picture on a cave wall to interpret. We want to know what our predecessors have felt, used or seen. We want to know the way life was.

The process requires a great deal of detective work. It takes a lot of time and in the end the inspectors are often left guessing what meaning may come from sketchy, incomplete sources. But, the hunt goes on. What happened? Who did what and why? How did they do it? And importantly, how did they feel about it?

The advances in technology have provided this generation a much easier way to provide some answers for tomorrow's generation. Because the word processor exists, we can write and revise with endless ease. Because of the digital photography, we can take our own photos, past and current, and embed them in our printed text. Because of the laser printer, we can print typeset quality documents. Because of print-on-demand technology, we can make these books available to the world. The upshot of it all is this: We can write a book about ourselves, affordably and in a relatively short period of time. Printed on acid-free paper and bound in a hardback cover, your personal life story is preserved in virtually everlasting condition. You can save the archeologist a lot of time.

What do we know of even the previous generation? What do you really know about your parents? Why did your father choose his occupation? What did he choose not to do and why? What extra activities did your mother participate in school? What did her teachers think of her? What was her dream before she married? What lasting effect did your father's father have on him? What did he think of his father and why? There are hundreds of questions that if asked and answered form a record that any child from any generation would be eager to read.

The idea of a personal biography is to preserve family history and family values. Genealogies record names and dates, but only a personal biography records what you did, why and how, and what you believed in. Only a personal biography tells who you are.

What is being called a "personal biography" here is sometimes called an oral history, sometimes an autobiography and sometimes a memoir. An oral history is called that because the process of creating a life story involves being interviewed and recorded. You can record yourself. Those notes or tapes are transcribed and edited into an easy-to-read format.

An autobiography may tell your story from beginning to end and comprehensively cover every phase of your life. A memoir may include select topics you want to focus on. The comprehensive autobiography and the selective memoir are both tried-and-true ways of creating a personal biography. What you choose to include is up to you.

Creating a personal biography is one of the best things you could ever do for the kids and the grandkids and the generations to come. Such a book only gains in value over time – until it becomes precious and priceless within the family.

We need to know something about our pasts, our roots, in order to know something about ourselves. Russell Baker, long-time New York Times columnist, wrote that, "…our children have the right to know from whence they came. So they know the stuff from which they are made." Even if we are made of "ordinary" stuff, we want to know it.

The miracle of DNA is now well known and we know in some detail how our human traits are passed on. Our crooked teeth, our proclivity for this or that disease, or our genius and talents can more or less be traced to the double helix in our cells. Even before the discovery of DNA, though, we already suspected that the newborn had dad's nose or mom's eyes.

It has not been so obvious, however, that our family culture is also passed on with the same traceability of the DNA compound. In Maury Bowen's well known text, Generation to Generation, he documented the recurring patterns of behavior that are passed on from one generation to the next. The often heard exclamation, "He's just like his father!," was typically taken seriously only in a moment of anger. Bowen documented that there really was something to it all.

Despite the protests heard from many an adolescent child, "I'll never be like my dad [or mother]," we tend to be remarkably similar. Reading the text of a father's personal biography, or even more illuminating, when reading the words of a great grandfather, the progeny of the forefathers are taken aback at some of the eerie similarities to be found.

To read about our ancestors is to read about ourselves. That's why we're all looking into the past. That's why we want to find the anonymous soldier's letter. We want to know his heart in the midst of terror or tedium. In his account of his moments, we seek to explain our own lives; we decipher our own past choices and find a forecast for our futures.

My grandfather, Francis Morrow, for example, played a valve trombone in the Morrow Brothers Quartet. It was made up of three brothers and a proxy, actually. They performed on the Chautauqua circuit, playing in tents in forty-six of the forty-eight states. We suspect they made it into Canada, too. We're not sure.

They played a brass quartet and sang four-part harmony and did comedy skits. We don't know the numbers they played. We don't know who sang what parts. We don't know what their comedy was about. We don't know their best song, their best joke, or the best town they ever played. We don't know. We haven't a word from him.

His daughter, my aunt, became an opera singer. She moved from Bement, Illinois to New York City and sang on the stage. She sang in Radio City Music hall when it was the place to play. She once roomed with the great prima donna of the day, Beverly Sills. She had music in her blood and she had to perform. Just like her father.

My brother wrote his first song at eight years old using a ukulele he taught himself how to play. He marched into the kitchen one day and sang us a set of songs he'd composed while shut behind the closed door of his bedroom – alone

Why Write a Personal Biography?

with his imagination and his undeniable urge to sing. He was compelled for some reason to make music.

My sister had the urge to play too, and joined my brother in forming a band that played all over the Midwest and beyond. My brother went on to write children's musicals and record in Nashville.

Now his daughter has made the violin her life's endeavor and plays first chair in a local orchestra and attends music camps all over the country.

What my grandfather's words might have meant! What force and inspiration they might have added to the legacy that so obviously rests in all their souls. Yet we have not a word from him.

A single page from Dead Sea Scrolls might not have had that much value the day they were completed, but just a piece of it would fetch a million dollars today. My grandfather's words would not be worth so much money, but in my family would have been worth a million heart beats where his memory is felt in what they do with their own lives, in the lives of his grand children, and great grandchildren, and great, great grand children and so on.

We pay thousands of dollars for life insurance premiums over a lifetime to provide a fortune for the well being of those we leave behind, but most fail to spend a dime recording a single thing we've said or thought or done.

To live seventy years is to live over 600,000 hours. To be summarized in the single line of an epitaph is inadequate. Was life so empty that there was nothing to say about it? NO. To spend a few hours summing it all up is not too much to spend on it.

But, my life is so... ordinary

It is an act of unselfish generosity to record how you have faced your challenges, to tell how you have worked and paid your way, supported your family, nurtured their wounds, celebrated their successes, grieved for your losses, shared your fortunes, laughed and cried – and perhaps you might have done it all without a single trophy on the mantle to show for it. But, it will be fascinating to your children, or some distant descendant's child a few generations down the road who will find comfort and pride in leading their own ordinary life. They will find it has meaning because one of their own persevered and had pride in a life lived earnestly, sincerely, and with goodness in your heart.

We need the connection today, more than ever. In an age where some unrelated rap singer has become a mentor to the children of an entire generation, we need grounding. We all need to know it, from whence we came. To know who we are and who we can be. When the day comes, when the children's curiosity is piqued, they'll have a book to pick up and words to read from their own bloodline. They will have something from their past to refer to and to light a path for their own future.

I believe your personal biography is a gift. It's something done about you, but not for you. And over the ages it only grows in value – progressing from the precious to priceless.

There is no substitute for the ability to slowly read and reread the written record. From a picture, we can guess at its meaning; from the written word we can know. We can know that our humanity has common threads. We can know that success and failure are inextricably related; two sides of the same coin every time.

The popular rendering of famous personalities can sometimes be misleading. The tale of the grandeur and the immortalizing effect of fame is distorting. We may hear of the famous person's bouts with their personal demons, but somehow it seems all surreal, as though their difficulties were a mistake. That such difficulty was something not meant for them. We still have difficulty digesting both sides of the coin of human existence.

But when the story is told about one of us, it seems believable and part of the ordinary fabric of life. We benefit by this balanced framing of expectations. When we read how the "ordinary" members of our ancestry suffer and succeed in those alternating waves of real life, we are heartened by it. We, too, know that we are suffering and succeeding no more or no less than what ought to be expected. Yet each of our stories has its own themes.

But, what is there to tell?
Some say that all the stories to be told have been told. Fiction writers, however, find endless combinations on the basic themes of life to tell. There will never be the last novel, because the uniqueness of our conditions is unlimited. So too is your story. It is necessarily unique and therefore worthy of telling.

In telling your own story, you may apply the overarching understanding you wish it to have. The facts, by themselves, do not explain themselves. You need a theme to find a voice for them. You may gather clusters of associated facts and provide a meaning to attach to the theme. It is up to you to frame your life, as the living author of your very own life in its original context -- the context you lived and understood like no other could.

But, I'm not sure I remember it well.
Did you know that false eyewitness identifications are the most conspicuous mistake in erroneous capital convictions?

Why Write a Personal Biography?

The Center on Wrongful Convictions at the Northwestern University School of Law looked at 86 death-row inmates who were cleared and found that faulty eyewitness identifications played a role in more than half of them-making them "by far the most ubiquitous factor."

The famous defense lawyer, Barry Scheck concludes that "Mistaken identification is the single greatest cause of the conviction of the innocent."

By 1979 there were over six hundred books written about the Kennedy assassination, all offering to shed some light on who was responsible for it. There was and is yet considerable difference of opinion on the matter.

The famous writer Dylan Thomas once said about his memory,

> "I can't remember whether it snowed six days and six nights when I was twelve or whether it snowed twelve days and twelve nights when I was six."

Your life story is not a trial. Nonetheless, we are all interested in being acquitted positively. I would suggest that nearly all, if not all of us, are deserving of a sympathetic summary, and you were the only regular eyewitness to your own life's events. It's up to you to speak up. Given enough detail, we can and do find sympathy where we sometimes never expected to find it. Your personal biography is your opportunity to provide the ample details of your life that only a person in your position could explain.

Since the cave man first etched a sketch of the world that laid beyond the cavern in which he dwelt, we have been trying to explain how it is and was. Some of their hieroglyphics have survived and anthropologists covet the secret knowledge they represent.

Why Write a Personal Biography?

Every one of us is an anthropologist too. We want to know how it was in the hopes of explaining how it is. We know there is a connection. We know that events are linked in a chain of, at least, loosely connected elements of cause and effect. We are inexorably interested on what begets what. What brings about love and hate? What brings about peace or war? What makes us want to live or die? What brings us hope?

As no stranger can provide the metaphysical meaning in an intimate lover's touch, no stranger can provide a clue to the mysteries of life like a member of the bloodline. The connection is automatically intimate. We sense it. And were more of our life stories recorded, we would know it better than just having a sense of it.

The basic challenge is to get it done, to get the story on paper. As clearly noble and needed as this project is, it is all too easy to put it off. The everyday tasks of life take a position at the top of our to-do list while the creation of this treasure gets put off. The time to act on this is when the inspiration has struck. Once the parent or grandparent is gone, the stories they had to tell goes away with them, forever.

Your contribution is, therefore, profound. In comparison to the anonymous art of the ancient caveman, your elaborated story gives the generations not just clues, not just facts, but interpretations and, therefore, meaning to life. Tell it. Write it. Help us all understand.

Will Anybody Read It?

"Only the mediocre are always at their best."

- Jean Giraudoux

So you may be thinking that the most interesting thing you ever wrote was your signature. Don't fret. Let's do a reality check. Who among us has not bothered to read the most vile etchings on a public restroom wall?

Point made. People will read anything, so stop worrying.

If I had reached for fame in any or every endeavor I've considered in my life, I would have never started anything. Eliminating grandiosity is the first thing a writer of anything must do.

Your story will be appreciated and widely read in the family if you typed it in Arabic. The family would have a ball decoding it. So just do your best.

Before You Write

"It is as difficult to live the good life as it is to write one."

-- Unknown

There are things you can do to establish what you'll want to tell about. The first is so obvious it can be overlooked. Something has inspired you with the idea of writing your memoir. Jot down all the ideas swirling around in your head in any order they come to mind. In the intense effort to write your story, it is too easy to forget some of the items that inspired you in the first place.

Next, use the available prompts you have to recall tales you'll want to include. Review the following items.

- Family photo albums
- Family documents
- Heirlooms and keepsakes
- Scrapbooks
- School year books

As you look at your family photos, make a note of tales that come to mind. Pictures of friends, vacations and family members can remind you of events surrounding that photo or simply trigger an association. Invite a family member or two to look with you. Two memories are better than one and you may be reminded of events by your partner.

Look at family documents such as:

- Certificates
- School report cards

- Deeds
- Military Discharge Papers
- Awards
- Divorce papers
- Correspondence
- Mortgage papers
- Legal papers

Any one of these types of documents may prompt a memory.

And be sure to tell everyone in the family and close friends about your project. Ask them outright for suggestions of things you might tell about. You may be pleasantly surprised with their recollections.

After documenting your basic family tree, reviewing the photo albums, the family's personal papers, family heirlooms and keepsakes, and after seeking suggestions from your relatives of what you might remember to tell, you will interview yourself.

Modes of Development

"Every journalist has a novel in him, which is an excellent place for it."

- Russel Lynes

Don't try to be a writer. Just write. This book is not meant for one who aspires to create a great novel. This is meant for those who simply want to write something the family will be pleased to read.

You might think of how you're going to approach the blank page before you begin, by considering the following three modes of development.

- Chronology
- Chronology & Topical
- Topical

Chronology
No life is so tidy that it can be fairly summarized by simply reciting a series of events, but using the timeline structure provides for a cogent presentation. Even with this proscribed progression, there will be events that lead up to occurrences that emanate outside the person – war, deaths, financial crisis, and motivations influenced by a convergence of factors that cannot always be easily synchronized with the timeline of your life experiences. Events from experiences from long past history may suddenly have bearing on your current life, for example. A court ruling may put an end to a career. A death in the family may leave emotional scars that don't reveal themselves until an associated event brings it to mind years later. Telling a life story is never entirely about a simple chronology of events.

Chronology & Topical

We have to tell one thing at a time, but it isn't absolutely necessary to maintain a forward progressing timeline that never retreats or flashes back to an earlier time already covered in your story. When the subject's life is divided into a composite of major endeavors – parenthood involving a severely ill child, abrupt career changes resulting from overwhelming outside forces, a remedial education aimed at a new avocation, or an election to village president, we might then suspend the straightforward chronology to travel each channel separately. We may follow a trail of public service from early adulthood to middle age then return to an earlier age to pick up another path about your home life or career. Such an approach places more emphasis on the themes of your life instead of merely the timeline.

Topical

The facts do not explain themselves. You need a theme to find a voice for them. Clusters of associated facts create a meaning to support a theme. Perhaps, you've always been a high-energy extrovert. Or maybe you've always been a very private person. Patterns can emerge as you recount your life.

We might abandon the birth to present time chronology altogether to explore special subjects. You might write about your life in your particular occupation. A life as a small town detective, for example, would have its own special facets.

Or one might write about a battle with disease or disability. Or a special journey, an investigation, life as a twin, as a volunteer or as a hobbyist. Such tales will focus on yourself, but inevitably become broadened by the discussion of the issue and the key participants in your story.

You may not have a clear idea how you will eventually organize the story when you start. It is most likely you won't. That's OK. I recommend you write your story in segments and assemble it later. That is the point where you will begin to choose your final structure and identify themes if you find them there.

Organizing the Information

"Get your facts first, then you can distort them as you please."

-- Mark Twain

One of the larger challenges you face in telling your story is getting your facts together. There needs to be some kind of order to them.

Segmenting the components of your life and exploring them in a chronological sequence may help keep your thoughts channeled and your story cogent. There will be some overlapping tales and sequences, and that is fine. Some repetition is necessary.

If you're using Microsoft Word to write your story, I suggest you write each event, episode or experience as a segment and save it in a separate file. I'll give you more tips about doing this in the *Indexing* section on page 23 and in the *Design And Layout* section beginning on page 89. Whether you're following a strict chronological timeline, a topical arrangement, or a mix of both, saving your segments in separate files like this gives you the flexibility to easily arrange them in the order you want them to be.

The following is a reasonably comprehensive list of categories you might choose to follow. Add any other categories that might tailor fit the story you have to tell. For example, you may have a large number of stories about the "War" or a "Trip Around the World." If it makes sense, then add a category. You will use these categories to label your segments and folders.

Organizing the Information

Categories
- Childhood
- Children
- Education
- Family of Origin
- Family
- Friends
- Fun
- Marriage
- Work
- Retirement
- Service
- Special Subjects (Creativity, Avocations, Medical, etc.)

Here are some topics you might explore in each category:

- Childhood
    - Best friends
    - Early interests
    - Early life-shaping experiences
    - First homes
    - Gifts
    - Health
    - Holidays
    - Learning experiences
    - Mealtimes
    - Personality
    - Pets
    - Special aptitudes
    - Special events

- Children
    - About the births of your children
    - Children and school life
    - Fun with the children
    - Gifts

- Health
- Holidays
- Learning experiences
- Life-shaping experiences
- Mealtimes
- Personalities
- Pets
- Special aptitudes
- Special events
- Things you taught your children

- Family of Origin
  - About close relatives
  - About mother and father's personalities
  - About you siblings' personalities
  - Closest sibling relationship
  - Gifts
  - Holidays
  - Mealtimes
  - Mother and father's rules of conduct
  - Mother and father's special interests
  - Places you've lived
  - Things mother and father taught you
  - Things you did together
  - Your parents' occupations
  - Your responsibilities in the family

- Education
  - School experiences
  - Schools
  - Social life
  - Studies

- Marriage and Relationships
  - About married life
  - Best times
  - Trials and tribulations
  - Gifts
  - Health

Organizing the Information

- Finances
- Quirks
- Balancing work and life
- Dating
- Divorce
- Living alone
- Meeting your spouse
- Remarriage
- Family after Children
    - Emancipating the children
    - Life without the children
- Work Life
    - Life at work
    - Preparing for a career
    - Your occupations
- Retirement Years
    - Future plans
    - Reflections on past years
- Service
    - Occupation
    - Places you served
    - Special experiences
- Special Subjects
    - Awards
    - Church leadership
    - Club membership
    - Extended health issues
    - Extraordinary losses or gains
    - Hobbies
    - Promotions
    - Public Office

Consider brainstorming some things to tell about before you begin and during the process. Sit out on the porch or by the pond some early morning before the day overtakes you. Let

Organizing the Information

your mind wander unfettered by the tasks of the day. Things will come to you.

Take a notebook and label each page with a category and a topic like those above. Examples: "Work life – welding apprenticeship," or "Childhood – the dog bite." Use a whole page for each one. Paper is cheap. This leaves you lots of room to add a keyword or phrase for each item you may include. You can even make a few detailed notes so your memory will be triggered when you get to that item in the writing process.

The Big Secret to Telling Your Story

"A blank page is God's way of showing you how hard it is to be God."

- Unknown

If you can ask yourself questions, you can write your story. All you have to do is answer them. How you put a sentence together is another matter, but the fact is, the family is most interested in substance. Just answer your own questions and you will have substance enough. And once it's read, the reader will feel well fed. So don't worry about making the New York Times Best Sellers list.

Asking and Answering the Questions
Journalists have been taught for years the age-old list of questions used to get to the bottom of a story. They are:

- What?
- When?
- Where?
- Who?
- How?
- Why?

The task of writing your story can seem daunting if it's seen as a creative writing project. Coming up with something interesting presents what seems to be an overwhelming task for many -- recalling a lifetime of experiences all at once and culling through them for those gold nugget tales. That's making the project far more difficult than it need be.

A small novel may be sixty thousand words. An interesting, well-told memoir may be twenty to thirty thousand words.

However, I suggest that you look at the project not in terms of how long the book will eventually be. I suggest that it will be quite enough if you simply use a basic outline of topics, as I have already suggested, then answer the questions you pose to yourself. Your story will come together with more ease than you might expect. Don't look up. Just ask and answer the questions and it will all come together.

With each new piece of your story, you want to make sure to set the stage for the reader. This is easy for a writer to overlook because you have the setting in your own mind as you write. A reader becomes frustrated when they're disoriented. They'll likely quit reading if they are.

Setting the Stage
Begin by telling us in a brief statement what happened. Like this:

1. I took the electrician's licensing exam.
2. I took my vacation.
3. I quit that job.
4. I found him alive.

That tells us what. Ask yourself where this happened, then tell the reader.

1. I took the electrician's licensing exam *in the Union Hall 303 conference room*.

2. I took my vacation *in Hawaii*.

3. I quit that job *in the foreman's office*.

4. I found him alive *behind the wheel of the car*.

Ask yourself when this happened.

1. I took the electrician's licensing exam in the Union Hall 303 conference room. *This was the first week after my*

apprenticeship was completed in May of 1959.

2. I took my vacation in Hawaii *in the spring of that same year*.

3. I quit that job in the foreman's office *on a Monday morning before the first break*.

4. I found him alive behind the wheel of the *car in the dark of night*.

Ask yourself who was involved.

1. I took the electrician's licensing exam in the Union Hall 303 conference room. This was the first week after my apprenticeship was completed in May of 1959. *Jack Quinlan, the regional secretary for our local, administered the test.*

2. I took my vacation in Hawaii in the spring of that same year. *Shel, my fishing buddy, his cousin Marty and I went together.*

3. I quit that job in the foreman's office on a Monday morning before the first break. *The foreman, my boss for the last five years, took the news badly.*

4. I found him alive behind the wheel of the car in the dark of night. *I was alone and had no idea who to call.*

The real intrigue in any story is how it happened and why. The headline of a news story usually tells us what happened, e.g., "Weapons Inspector Found Dead." Such a story almost always tells us the victim's name and when he was found. But, what we most want to know is how this happened and why? Was he murdered? Or was it a suicide? Why would anyone want him dead? Why would he want to kill himself? How did things reach this state of affairs? You will give interest to your story by telling us the how and why of your events and episodes.

Continuing with our examples, ask yourself how this happened.

1. I took the electrician's licensing exam in the Union Hall 303 conference room. This was the first week after my apprenticeship was completed in May of 1959. Jack Quinlan, the regional secretary for our local, administered the test.

    I had studied every manual the local had given me to study, but most of my learning came from my on the job training with Mort Anderson who taught me everything from splicing to circuits.

2. I took my vacation in Hawaii in the spring of that same year. Shel, my fishing buddy, Marty his cousin and I went together. *We drove Shel's 1959 Cadillac fourteen hours to the coast.*

3. I quit that job in the foreman's office on a Monday morning before the first break. The foreman, my boss for the last five years, took the news badly. *I laid my badge on the desk and told him no amount of money was worth risking my life up on that rig in a windstorm.*

4. I found him alive behind the wheel of the car in the dark of night. I was alone and had no idea who to call. *I had felt my way in the dark until I found the door handle on the driver's side. I opened the door and blindly felt around until my hand came to rest on Del's side.*

And now, tell the most important part of the story you can tell. Ask yourself why this happened the way it did.

1. I took the electrician's licensing exam in the Union Hall 303 conference room. This was the first week

after my apprenticeship was completed in May of 1959. Jack Quinlan, the regional secretary for our local, administered the test.

I had studied every manual the local had given me to study, but most of my learning came from my on the job training with Mort Anderson who taught me everything from circuits to junction boxes.

There was no choice in the matter. With all the out of work electricians in the area, those most likely to get a job were the licensed electricians.

2. I took my vacation in Hawaii in the spring of that same year. Shel, my fishing buddy, his cousin Marty and I went together. We drove Shel's 1959 Cadillac fourteen hours to the coast. *We would have flown if we'd had the money, but we lost most of what we had in the poker game the night before.*

3. I quit that job in the foreman's office on a Monday morning before the first break. The foreman, my boss for the last five years, took the news badly. I laid my badge on the desk and told him no amount of money was worth risking my life up on that rig in a windstorm. *I'd seen two men injured on this job taking risks this foreman should never have asked anyone to do. I wasn't going to be the next.*

4. I found him alive behind the wheel of the car in the dark of night. I was alone and had no idea who to call. I had felt my way in the dark until I found the door handle on the driver's side. I opened the door and blindly felt around until my hand came to rest on Del's side. *If I hadn't looked for him, no one would have. Because I found him, he lived.*

The Big Secret to Telling Your Story

The secret to writing your story lies in your ability to ask yourself questions. The easy part is answering them. Of course, it's up to you to choose what's important to ask yourself about, but don't be too cautious. Real life is about real things and not many of them are of hair-raising importance. But an accumulation of details paints a picture and gets the reader involved in the story by orienting them. I suggest you focus on telling what you thought was important to you, not what you think is going to strike the reader as important. Don't worry about what the reader will think about the story, just do a good job of telling the story and let the chips fall where they may.

Painting your Personality

Use these questions to draw out your knowledge, values and desires. All this paints a picture of your personality. The reader wants to know what you're like. How you approach your life's challenges as well as how you look back on them is the heart of your story.

- What were your alternatives at the time?
    - Why did you choose what you chose?
    - What did you expect?
    - What went in to making your choice?
- What is the difference between your circumstance before and after you made the change/choice? Why is that important?
- How did you feel about it then and now?
- How did this change your life?
- What difference has this made in you?
- What did you learn / take away from that experience?

Exercise: Use these pages to write three follow up questions you would ask this writer having read the following paragraphs.

The Big Secret to Telling Your Story

Example #1

"After working twenty years for McDonald's Corporation, I decided that the life of an independent consultant is what I wanted. I negotiated a severance package that granted me six months income. With that income I could begin the marketing of my services."

Example #2

"When I found out my daughter's grades had fallen to such low levels, I was presented with a difficult situation. A non-custodial parent works by remote control at best. I had no real idea what Mary's (my daughter) reading, math or study skills were. I simply knew I had to do something."

Example #3

"My grandfather spent the last weeks of his life sleeping on a twin bed in our dining room. We all played a part in his care. I fed him a watery mix of oatmeal for his breakfast before leaving for school. At nights, I read him passages from the Bible. He passed away one spring morning with the sun shining through the window above his bed."

Suggested Questions:

Example #1

"After working twenty years for McDonald's Corporation, I decided that the life of an independent consultant is what I wanted. I negotiated a severance package that granted me six months income. With that income I could begin the marketing of my services."

- Why did you want to leave McDonald's?
- What was appealing about being an independent consultant?

- How did you feel about starting a new career with limited resources to operate on?

Example #2

"When I found out my daughter's grades had fallen to such low levels, I was presented with a difficult situation. A non-custodial parent works by remote control at best. I had no real idea what Mary's (my daughter) reading, math or study skills were. I simply knew I had to do something."

- Why had your daughter's grades fallen?
- What does it mean to operate "by remote control?"
- Why did you not know what your daughter's skills were?

Example #3

"My grandfather spent the last weeks of his life sleeping on twin bed in our dining room. We all played a part in his care. I fed him a watery mix of oatmeal for his breakfast before leaving for school. At nights, I read him passages from the Bible. He passed away one spring morning with the sun shining through the window above his bed."

- How did your grandfather respond to you when you tended to him?
- What Bible passages did you choose to read and why?
- How did you feel when your grandfather passed away?

Exercise: Use the questions above to tell about the following items.

- Tell about the first job you took.
- Tell about the schoolwork you were given in grade school.

- Tell about the time you got your driver's license.

Adding Definition

You can better describe your authentic self by contrasting yourself to relatives or even a hypothetical personality, and to paths not taken. In the same way black letters on a page show up best against a white paper background, your personality is most discernable when contrasted to options not taken or in contrast to how others viewed your choices.

In exploring your choices, ask yourself these questions:

- How would somebody else have handled this?
- What did others recommend?
- How am I different than my dad/mother/brother/sister/friend/associate in the way I handled this?

Listen to this writer's explanation of why he avoided service in the Viet Nam War.

> "I didn't go to Viet Nam. I was in school with a college deferment for most of those years. After I graduated, I joined the National Guard. The war ended before I was discharged after six years of service."

The Viet Nam War years were a tumultuous time. For those who lived in that period, particularly those who were asked to fight in the war, it was an emotionally challenging time. The subject begs for some explanation.

One could and should provide your personal reasoning for your choices. This is what this writer tells us.

> "I had read all there was to read about the history of the Viet Nam conflict as a part of my college studies. I knew the French had tried and failed to convert the country to the Catholic faith. I knew they had economic interests that led them to colonialize the

> country. And I knew they had been defeated militarily in trying to maintain their hold. It was clear to me that a Western nation had no hope of controlling Viet Nam for any reason. I wasn't going to be fodder for a president's fancy or another failed policy."

This tells us what the writer thought. But, no decision is made in a vacuum. To add interest and the appropriate context to the weight of this decision, one might include the opinion of another who might have had some influence on your choice. This is what this writer's father thought about the matter.

> "My father was reserved about it, but he completely disagreed with me. Dad had served in World War II. He had shot at the enemy's soldiers with the intent to kill and had. He wasn't proud about the killing. I thought his face showed his unspoken regrets when he told me about it. He didn't want to kill, but his country had called him when the world was up for grabs. Hitler was on the loose and he was a madman. He told me the United States waited far too long to join in the war, that Hitler had almost succeeded. He thought each individual soldier could not make that decision – to go to war or not. You had to trust your country and go when called. He wasn't angry with me. He just thought I was terribly wrong, and once we had discussed it we left the subject alone."

Now we know something about the internal debate this man had in deciding to avoid the war the way that he did. He didn't exactly defy his country, but his intent was to stay out of the war. He chose a middle ground, college deferments and the National Guard. Maybe we can begin to see why he did not choose to run to Canada or burn his draft card as others did. Perhaps, it was his father's quiet objection hanging in the back of his mind that guided him towards the choices he made.

The Big Secret to Telling Your Story

The writer shows the difference between himself and another. He shows the contrasting philosophies of how two different people approached this difficult matter. One may understand both viewpoints and develop empathy for the writer and what he went through in making his choice.

Does this writer have the courage of his convictions? Does this writer consider his choices carefully or was he careless? Is this writer narrow minded or can he understand another point of view while still disagreeing with it? Does this writer come from a family background where family love persevered through an agonizing and volatile issue that might have split other families?

Providing this definition of the writer's choices in contrast to competing opinions adds color and depth to his personality and its shaping influences. And it makes a better story.

Consider how this young man decided to take a job rather than continue playing on his high school basketball team.

> "I decided to take a job at the Tolly's, the neighborhood grocery store. Tolly's was a family owned grocery and felt like it. It had a clean but weathered interior that made the store feel homey unlike the chain stores felt with their antiseptic floors and bright lighting. I thought I would feel comfortable working there."

Now we know why he chose what he did. But, what alternatives did he pass up in making this choice? Life is a series of trade-offs. We give up this to get that at every turn. The opportunity exists in describing this choice by contrasting his choice to the alternatives. His reasoning will become clearer and more vivid. Telling the reader what this young man gave up to get this job will reveal more of his personality.

> "I decided to give up my fledgling basketball career at Stephen Decatur High School for the pursuit of money, mainly. College was only two years away and I had no real idea how I could afford it. Although a part-time job bagging groceries was not likely to pay all my tuition, I had to do something figuring all would work out eventually.
>
> And I was never confident in my basketball skills either. Following on the heels of our teams who had won a first, third and fourth places finishes in the state tournament, left me quaking in the wake of some very good players. I didn't have the feeling I would make a good showing and preferred to skip what I thought was going to be a failed and embarrassing experiment."

The writer tells us that his decision was one part optimistic practicality and one part faltering pessimism. The two contrasting elements of his choice paint a colorful picture of this writer's way of approaching life.

Starting Anywhere, Going Anywhere

Marriage and family counselors learn to start where the clients want to start in telling their story. It's not only logical; it's the only way possible. Trying to guide a client to a new perspective necessarily must follow a review of their original thoughts. In each succeeding session, the counselor must find out where the client is today before proceeding.

Yet in writing, some may try to be too controlling over their own efforts to tell their story. You can try starting at the beginning and continuing to the end of your story. If it works for you, do it.

But, just like clients come to the counselor's office with something on their minds to say, so you will sit before the recorder or word processor with something on your mind. My recommendation is to start there, with what's on you mind at the moment. Start every day, every writing session that way.

What's on your mind is what you most care about, at least at the moment, and there is where you'll find the passion to tell your story and all its details. If you try to adhere to a strict outline, I believe you'll choke off a wellspring of inspiration. Or, worse, you may forget to tell it at all.

For that same reason, I believe in jotting down a note of any story that comes to mind that you want to tell. So when you're in the car or on the train or sitting at the breakfast table, find some way to make a keyword note of it. Leave yourself a voice message. Put a sticky note in your shoe. Write it on the palm of your hand. Or you risk losing it.

Indexing

If you're going to be a professional biographer, you can take this organizing effort to its finest measures. I'm writing this book for the rest of us. I suggest again that you write your story in segments and record each one in a separate file on your computer. If you're doing this by hand, bless your heart, title each page with a category and a subtitle.

If you're handwriting your personal biography, begin a segment by labeling the page with one of the following titles you'll find familiar. Then add a specific label for the segment you're writing.

I'm going to tell you how to assemble all these files in Microsoft Word, the most common authoring tool on the planet at present. It's easier to compile files in other programs like Adobe's FrameMaker and PageMaker, or QuarkXpress, for example, but that's another learning curve. But it all can be done in Word, and that's what most people own. So that's what I'll talk about in the *Design and Layout* chapter beginning on page 107.

Categories
- Childhood
- Children
- Education
- Family of Origin
- Family
- Friends
- Fun
- Marriage
- Work
- Service
- Special Subjects: Creativity, Avocations, Medical

If you're handwriting your story, label your pages so it will be easier to assemble them later. The following are some examples:

Sample Label	Brief Description of the Segment
Family of Origin – Dad's dog house	How dad built a doghouse for my first pet puppy.
Work – Leaving the hardware store	The decision to switch from store manager to manufacturer's rep.
Marriage – Second child	How our second child was born.
Work – Bonus payment	Earning enough for the first home down payment.
Special Subject – Making a chest	Using dad's tools to make a chest.

If you're using Word, you'll only need to use the specific sub-label as the filename. You'll be creating folders with the category names to put them in.

What If I Can't Remember?

"A little inaccuracy can sometimes save tons of explanation."

- H.H. Munro (Saki)

The truth is we can't entirely remember what we've witnessed with a manner of seconds or minutes of what we've seen. College classrooms around the nation seem to prove this point over and over again by staging a surprise event in the classroom then polling the class for the details. Class members get all kinds of things wrong – the race of the offender, the gender, whether there was a gun involved, what they said and more. The value of an eyewitness is reduced by chilling proportions once an experiment like this is performed.

Prosecutors are fond of the eyewitness. They believe them to be, for their purposes, irrefutable sources of truth. Defense attorneys, however, are twenty times more likely to call experts on the validity of eyewitness testimony than prosecutors.

The debate rages around the effects of time lapse, original awareness, motivations and stress and a host of other factors on the reliability of eyewitness testimony. All of it points to the frailty of eyewitness accounts. So, who are you to check with to corroborate your facts? It's not easy to get the facts.

As a marriage and family counselor, I had the frequent occasion to hear competing versions of an event. And as was often the case, both parties wanted a favorable adjudication from me.

But I, like the reader of your memoirs, didn't hold the authority or the omniscience to pass such a judgment. In any case, it hardly mattered whose version was more "accurate," as though that were possible. My suggestion was that had there been a video camera and a sound recording, the two parties would not have interpreted the situation similarly anyhow.

At the very moment life is transpiring before us, it is most likely that we will not see it the same way another has. We all see the world though the lens of our own world view. And what may look like anger to one looked like humor to another. At age six, the dog was huge. Now, the dog would seem small, and so on.

One college class experimented with the interpretations of scenes from television sitcoms. Individuals were asked to view the same program and their laughter was recorded. After the show, participants were asked to explain what made them laugh. The differences between viewers were surprisingly disparate. It makes you wonder if the screenwriter really knew what makes the viewer laugh.

Standup comics test their new material before live audiences trying to determine what the good jokes are. No comic intends to write a joke that's not funny. The spouse or close friend of the comic may laugh at it and call it funny. But some, most or all of any given audience may not find it funny. Our responses can be quite different to the same act.

Your effort to tell your story is not aimed at deceiving the reader. You may be comfortable, in my opinion, making your best effort to portray your story as best you can, with the recall you can muster, to depict what an experience meant or seemed like to you. Your response to the setting the very day it happened may not have been entirely "accurate" to begin with.

I don't suggest you make up anything. And I don't suggest that you hedge every recollection with the subjunctive… "it

What If I Can't Remember?

might have been..." or, "as best as I can recall." If the fact is material and would likely change the meaning substantially, you might explain the limitation of your recall. If not, whether she wore a corsage is not critical. Do your best, that's good enough.

The Difference Is in the Details

"Writing is easy. All you do is stare at the blank sheet of paper until beads of blood form on your forehead."

- Gene Fowler

Let Shakespeare have his glory. I'm going to show you simple ways that any non-writer can use to raise the interest in his work above the level of graffiti. Kilroy is not going to show you up.

Adding Details

Stories become interesting when we read the details. The biography that reports I was born, worked and am sure to die is a bit too lean.

Reciting the sequence of events will be the easier part. Providing the interesting details is more challenging. Let me emphasize that the "details" provide the interest. What may seem to you to be common information, or boring minutiae is really what the reader wants. They do want to know what your mother's best meal was or dad's favorite joke. Tell details. Risk telling too much. You won't. And besides, you can trim the fat later if you feel it necessary.

Read this portion of a Civil War soldier's letter.

> The food is very plain, hard bread and salt pork, mainly. Once in a while we get something special like rice and dried potatoes, sometimes a little coffee and sugar. A few days ago we drew some soft bread, potatoes and onions. My shanty is made of pine logs. It is six feet wide and ten feet long with a place for a fireplace. It is five feet high to the eaves, and is covered with thick cotton cloth. My bed is softened with "Uncle Sam's Feathers", pine

The Difference Is in the Details

> branches. We sleep five in here. I am plenty weary from all the marching. If this is doing any good, I can't be sure. Sunday is not respected here at all. I have not heard but two sermons since I got here. We have no Chaplain which I regret. This is how we all live here.

This may not be the stuff of great novels, but I guarantee any family member of any generation would be pleased. All that ordinary detail, "hard bread" and "salt pork" and such may have seemed too ordinary to mention at the time. But, now, and I suspect even then, every detail was a delicious morsel.

Read the following information I extracted from an obituary notice published my local paper. (The names have been changed.)

> "Dr. Robert Smith, member of the faculty of the Allen B. Brown School for 24 years prior to his retirement in 1996, died in his hometown today. He is the author of "The Anglican Movement, Social Reformers in the 1950's" A passionate advocate of justice and civil liberties, he received his B.A. from the University of Illinois and his M.A. from the University of Chicago. Call for funeral plans at …"

A whole host of questions are inspired by just this minimal information.

- Why was he moved to write this book? What led up to that?
- What troubles did he have writing the book?
- How was it received?
- What did he think of what he wrote as he looked back on it?

- What did he teach at the Allen B. Brown School? Who did he teach? What did he consider important about it? What would he have done differently?
- Whose life did he most affect by what he's taught or wrote?
- How did the family feel about the causes he thought important?
- What was the greatest difficulty he faced in his life?

And so much more...

Or this one...

> "Dianne Smith was a resident of Chicago and North Miami Beach, Florida. Dianne was a hair stylist at the North Miami Beach Hotel. Later she became a Board Member of the State of Illinois Examiners Commissioners. Dianne retired to North Miami Beach, Florida where she spent much of her time playing golf and in several social clubs."

Think of the tales Ms. Smith has heard as a hairdresser in both Chicago and Miami.

- How were the people different in Chicago and Miami?
- What did clients talk about the most?
- How did talking to you help?
- How did you help your clients?
- Why did you become a Board Member of the Illinois Examiners Commissioners?
- What did you do there?
- What was the most difficult matter you faced?

The Difference Is in the Details

Of course, there's a whole life to talk about, but in just a single summary paragraph, the opportunity to compose at least one very interesting chapter clearly exists.

When you begin to add detail, you will find that you open the doors to memories that matter. The subtleties and facets of your life and your choices take on shape. The reader will begin to identify with you and the situation, and it makes for good reading.

Telling What Happened

"There are two kinds of people, those who finish what they start and so on."

- Robert Byrne

If you can ask yourself questions and answer them, you can tell your life story. Here's a sample.

Question: What was your first home like?

Describe it with as much detail as you can bear. Was it wood or brick? One story or two? Where was it on the block - on the corner? Next to what? New or old? How did it feel inside - warm or cold, bright or dark? What was special about it – a third generation home? What didn't you like about it – the noise in the neighborhood? What was the yard like – rusty old cars in the lawn? Who maintained the house and yard – your job? Describe the rooms, your room. What happened while you lived there – your high school years?

When an event is mentioned, ask yourself this sequence of questions?

- What happened? What did you expect to happen at the beginning?
- What led up to what happened?
- Where did it happen?
- How did it happen?
- Who did what?
- Why did you do/choose what you did? Why did others recommend or do what they did?
- What was the result?

- Looking back on it, what was important about it? How did you feel about it then and now? What did you learn from it?

Take your time and tell the story. Each little piece put together will make up the tapestry of the larger tale. Tell the little stories, and the big story will come out well.

Exercise: Get out your cassette recorder and record your recollection of the first time you had to perform something before a group – a recital, a book report, a speech, bagging groceries, your turn at bat? (Find it awkward to talk "to yourself" like that? Place a picture of a loved one on the table in front of you and talk to him or her as you tell it. Or, you could talk to the cat. Just don't be discouraged by her lack of interest.)

Persons, Places and Things

Tell Me Three Things About It

Use this simple rule to prime your memory and add interest to your tale. Whenever you first mention a person, place or thing, provide the reader with three details about it. Like this:

A Place

Original:

   "I was born at 145 Maple Street, Downers Grove, Illinois."

With Three Details:

   "I was born at 145 Maple Street, Downers Grove, Illinois. Our home was a small, wood-framed house located on a corner lot."

Small. Wood-framed. Corner lot.

Just three details make this beginning a more interesting story. You could stop there and have much improved a dry sounding sentence. But, what would happen if you added three more details?

Then, Tell Us Three More Things
With Three More Details

"I was born at 145 Maple Street, Downers Grove, Illinois. Our home was a small, wood-framed house located on a corner lot. My father and I painted it bright white in the middle of one hot summer. It was one of the rare times I got to spend so much time with Dad. I remember starting out with the greatest exuberance. The heat slowed me to a halt in no time. I was soaked with sweat, dry-mouthed and exhausted. It was then my Dad offered me this piece of wisdom. "A slow and steady pace is a better pace for a long project. You'll make fewer mistakes and get more done." After that, I stepped slower, took more breaks and before I knew it the first side was finished and I was still feeling able to continue."

You and your dad painted it. White. During a hot summer.

These three details create a scene for us to imagine – you and dad carrying ladders and paint cans around the house and such. But, here's the really important result of trying to add details: *it triggered a memory*. That's what can happen.

It opened up the remembrance of some advice your dad gave you that he felt was important. Maybe that advice is something you've followed all your life ever since. If so, add that to your story.

And maybe you'll want to tell us how your dad applied his philosophy to some other meaningful task that impressed you. Is that the way he approached his job too? Was this a big difference between how your dad versus your mother approached tasks? What was the difference?

Was there a reason why you chose white? Who chose it? Was there a difference of opinion about it? Was it always white? Was it the only white house on the block? Was there anything at all important about the house being white? If so, then tell us.

By telling the reader about these things, we get the idea of who you are and how you were shaped. And it all came out because the few details you added provoked the next questions.

Add three details at a time until you feel the scene has been exhausted, then move on to the next.

A Person

Original

"Stu Banner came to work about noon and left by two on the days he showed up. "

With Three Details

"Stu was short, five feet five, tops. In the warm months, he came to work clothed in a golf tee shirt unbuttoned at the collar to the last button to show his deep tan."

Short. Unbuttoned golf shirt. Tanned. This is better. But, of the three things the writer has told us now, we have reason to develop some curiosity. What effect did his height have on him? And why is he deeply tanned?

Then, Tell Us Three More Things

"Stu was short, 5 feet 5 tops. In the warm months, he came to work clothed in a golf tee shirt, unbuttoned to the last button to show his deep tan. He was so short there seemed to be no bend to his back and he tended to waddle like a penguin. Like they say about some short men, he seemed to have to prove his masculinity. That's why he wore his shirt unbuttoned as he did. It was his attempt at being sexy and it framed a large gold chain he always wore.

"He spent most of his time on his boat out on Lake Michigan. That's where he got his tan. And his girl friends. He had a series of girlfriends. He paraded each new catch through the office like she were a trophy. I don't know what attracted them, the collar or the boat, but I suspect the latter."

He was short *and* waddled like a penguin. The open collar was supposed to be sexy. He got his tan (and his girlfriends) on his boat.

These three added details led to some explanation and some observations. Stu seems to have been something of a playboy who found his self-esteem in getting a new girlfriend regularly. We have a better understanding of the writer's work environment knowing these things.

A Thing

Original

"We bought the painting in Peru. Later she framed it and hung it in the living room. The unconventional frame drew a lot of attention to it. Visitors almost always commented on it. I always liked it for the memory it held and because it was uniquely framed."

With three details

"We bought the painting in the city of Cuzco in Peru. There were a number of street vendors selling

> watercolor paintings. The picture was dramatically
> deep-set in a four-inch wide fluted frame. We hung it
> in the living room. The unconventional frame drew a
> lot of attention to it. Visitors almost always
> commented on it. I always liked it for the memory it
> held and because it was uniquely framed."

It was purchased in Cuzco. It was purchased from a street vendor. It was framed in a wide, fluted frame. We know more and it's getting interesting.

Then, Tell Us Three More Things

> "We bought the painting in the city of Cuzco in Peru.
> Cuzco is the oldest city in the Western Hemisphere
> and is located near the Macchu Pichu ruins. There
> were a number of street vendors selling watercolor
> paintings of ancient Cuzco scenes like the one we
> purchased.
>
> Later she framed it with a deeply beveled frame we
> found in a resale shop and refinished. The picture was
> dramatically deep-set in a four-inch wide fluted frame.
> We hung it in the living room. The unconventional
> frame drew a lot of attention to it. Visitors almost
> always commented on it. I always liked it for the
> memory it held and because it was uniquely framed."

It was bought in the *ancient* town of Cuzco. Cuzco is not just any town and this fact adds color to the description. It was a watercolor of an ancient scene. The picture was of a particular type of scene taken from this ancient setting. It was in a dramatic frame purchased in an unusual way. The frame was of an unusual kind and has had a personal touch added to it. It seems that this painting held the special memory surrounding the place where it was purchased and care was taken to make the painting special and it worked. Everyone commented on it. The added details make this painting much more special to the reader than as described in the original version.

Add three details to the sentences below based on your own life experience. Then add three more if you can. Let your powers of association add any experience to the details as they occur to you.

- My dad bought me my first bicycle.
- Mrs. Smith (whoever) was my first grade (any grade) teacher.
- I applied for my first job at...
- The classrooms looked like...
- During that vacation, we enjoyed (fill in the blank) the most.
- My best friend was ...

Choices, Changes, Gains and Losses

Telling About Who You Are

You can largely reveal to the reader who you are by explaining your choices, your expectations, and your reflections on the results of your choices. Making a choice mean things changed. When things change you feel a gain or a loss from it to some small or larger degree. Tell about the difference it made.

Sometimes gain or loss is thrust upon you, a birth or a death, an inheritance or a catastrophe. That, too, is worth telling about because it forces the individual to make choices given the new circumstances.

When you faced a change or a choice you made in life, tell the reader how you felt about it.

Mad, Sad or Glad

Many people find it difficult to identify their emotions surrounding many matters. Asked directly, "How do you feel about this or that?" many of us lock up unable to identify anything but what we thought. Part of that puzzling question comes from trying to be too accurate about the answer. Sometimes an accurate answer seems too revealing. Sometimes there are so many feelings that it's hard to pick one out.

Start with picking out one emotion of this simple threesome. I was mad, sad or glad. Using these broad terms, tell us how you felt at the beginning of a change or when you faced a choice. Then tell the reader how you felt afterwards or much later.

Telling us the feelings around a matter reveals your humanity and gives the reader something to identify with. Some may feel that having any emotion associated with any change is an expression of weakness. It is charged that many males particularly may think so. Nothing could further from the truth or the reality. Everyone feels something; it can't be stopped.

Using the mad, glad or sad labels gives those who have difficulty stating a feeling a launching point. You can refine the feeling later, but give it a label to begin with.

Original

> "I graduated high school in 1956 and began to think of where I would go next."

With an emotion attached

> "I graduated high school in 1956 and began to think of where I would go next. Graduating left me feeling a little sad. The prospect of moving on and leaving behind my friends, Brad and Doug left me wondering

just what I would do with my spare time. For four great years, the three of us had kept one another occupied with all kinds of fun and shenanigans."

He felt sad. This added detail naturally leads the writer to tell us why because stating that he was sad begs the question, "Why?" Now we want to know, "What 'fun and shenanigans'?" The story naturally unfolds and what you were like as a high school aged person can be told in context readers will find interesting. Characters have been added. There's activity to be explained.

Here's a list of changes common to many of us that would lend itself to an emotion you would naturally feel and could explain.

Education
- Going to school for the first time
- Leaving grade school and going to junior high school
- Leaving junior high school and going to high school
- Leaving high school and going to college
- Picking one college over another
- Picking a major in college
- Changing a major in college
- Beginning an internship
- Ending an internship

Relationship
- Leaving one girl or boyfriend for another
- Getting engaged
- Breaking an engagement
- Getting married
- Getting divorced
- Beginning a friendship
- Ending a friendship
- Changing from one group of friends to another group

Telling What Happened

Occupations
- Leaving one job for another
- Starting a business
- Selling a business
- Accepting a promotion
- Being transferred to a new job
- Being transferred to a new location
- Training in new job skills
- Being terminated
- Being laid off
- Joining the military
- Leaving the military

Gains and Losses
- Losing a loved one
- Having a child
- Losing a large sum of money
- Losing one's health
- Receiving an inheritance
- Receiving an insurance settlement
- Being involved in a lawsuit
- Having a near death experience

There are more than could possibly be listed in their entirety.

You may sooner than later find that the mad, sad and glad alternatives are too restrictive. Use your word processor's thesaurus (or get a book of synonyms) to make finer choices. You may be more than mad; you may have been furious – or only perturbed. You can find the just right word eventually, but start with these three simple choices to help yourself get started in identifying how you felt about things.

Tip: In Microsoft Word, point to the word you would like to change, then right-click to display a shortcut menu. Choose *Synonyms* from the list and review the list of alternatives. Click on the replacement word you like and the change will be made.

Emotional Integrity

"The young man who has not wept is a savage; the old man who will not laugh is a fool."

- George Santayana

The matter of emotional integrity is something often addressed in relationship counseling. It revolves around one party to the relationship camouflaging one's feelings, especially when suffering what feels like an injury to one's sensibilities. It's about hiding the hurt when you're truly hurt. Or hiding the anger when you're truly angry. Hiding feelings creates a fraudulent atmosphere for the relationship. The other party is kept in the blind and not offered the opportunity to adjust or apologize. The offended party lives with a festering beef.

The trick is to know when to let the little stuff go and when to be revealing. It is also about the diplomacy of revealing hurt feelings. Beginning with name calling, for example, gets undesirable results.

Likewise, one needs to learn how to accept such revelations with an open-minded desire to resolve the matter. Firing back with tit for tat diatribes doesn't help things either.

It is almost universally agreed that writing down one's most heated feelings for the purpose of mailing a complaint to the offender is a bad idea. You can't get the words back. And you can't amend the words in process as you can in a conversation where you can fluidly restate and refine your point. In conversation, you can benefit from the advantage of being able to add tone, touch and body language to soften the point. In writing, there is none of that advantage.

Emotional Integrity

To give your story the air of authenticity and validity, you need to observe the fundamental principle of emotional integrity. The reader has to know something of how you felt about the occurrences in your life. I have suggested the mad, sad, or glad trio of descriptives as a way of approaching the issue.

Consider the different affects of these paragraphs told with and without emotional integrity.

Without Emotion

> "The failure of the mill had a domino effect in the industry. My business of four years was among the first to close. I sold my inventory to the largest supplier in the area, my main competitor, for twenty cents on the dollar. By August, I was job hunting again."

With Emotion (Sad)

> "The failure of the mill had a domino effect in the industry. My business of four years was among the first to close. *When I closed the shop door for the last time, I felt a hollowness inside me as though I had not eaten in a week. I remember fumbling with the key trying to lock the door. I admit my eyes were teared up so I couldn't see the lock. I hadn't felt that miserable since my dog, Tiki, died when I was seven. It was devastating.* I sold my inventory to the largest supplier in the area, my main competitor, for twenty cents on the dollar. By August, I was job hunting again."

Your children and your children's children need not be spared the realities of defeat and disappointment. To dryly mention that a fledgling business had been snuffed out by circumstances and to glibly mention that this unfortunate businessman had to start again on something new robs the reader of a glimpse into real life. Just tell it like it was. Include your feelings.

Without Emotion

> "Shannon walked across the stage and took her degree from the Dean with one hand and shook his hand with the other. She graduated with a degree as a Registered Nurse."

With Emotion (Glad)

> "Shannon walked across the stage and took her degree from the Dean with one hand and shook his hand with the other. *She took one step with the degree in hand and paused to look out at the crowd where I sat. She raised the degree in her hand high above her head, smiled and waved at me as though we both had accomplished something. It had been a long, sometimes very difficult trail for the both of us. I was elated.* She graduated with a degree as a Registered Nurse."

Let's tell it like it is. Any parent who has watched their child receive the rewards of her effort is proud of the child and is inclined to give her the credit due. And every parent knows they too have had a hand in it. To expose the feelings a parent might have at a moment like this is enlightening to some readers and validating to others. Let the reader share in your authentic feelings of such a moment.

These tales tell the reader of honest feelings about loved one and one's self. It's another matter to begin to speak of your feelings towards others when the feelings are not positive.

I urge caution in expressing anything but the most tepid feelings towards others you may mention if the feeling is negative. Inflamed rhetoric seems to backfire on the writer. I could speculate why, but I would ask that you reflect how you have responded to invectives in print. I think we are all made a little uncomfortable reading what seems a little too heated. It frustrates the reader will want to hear the "other

Emotional Integrity

side of the story" when the case is made too hard. I generally suggest milder tones.

Here's how Mark Twain delivered his condemnation of a former publisher, Elijah Bliss, whom he thought swindled him repeatedly. After Bliss died, Twain said,

> "He has been dead a quarter of a century now. My bitterness against him has faded away and disappeared. I feel only compassion for him and if I could send him a fan I would."

If we all had the wit of Twain, we might try venting our hard feelings with such a humorous statement. The rest of us will simply have to try to be reserved about it.

Examples

Hot: I thought he was rotten human being.

Mild: I thought his actions were terribly unfair.

Hot: What she said was a pack of lies.

Mild: I found no supporting facts in what she said.

Hot: It was the ugliest picture in the display.

Mild: The picture didn't compare favorably with the others.

Compare these two passages of a not entirely happy event. The writer was mad about the turn of events, but restrained himself from making it a personal attack on his old coach.

Without Emotion

> "Bill and I scored forty points between us, over half the final score, and we won. That was twenty points better than our usual performance throughout the season. Herb

Williams usually contributed twenty or more, but his injury left him on the bench for the second half.

"The following day the paper quoted Coach Rizzert praising Herb's season long performance, but didn't mention our timely performance. Nonetheless, we were state champions in 1961."

With Emotion

"Bill and I scored forty points between us, over half the final score, and we won. That was twenty points better than our usual performance throughout the season. Herb Williams usually contributed twenty or more, but his injury left him on the bench for the second half.

"The following day the paper quoted Coach Rizzert praising Herb's season long performance, but didn't mention our timely performance. *Coach always preached team play and the value of everyone's contribution. I thought this was certainly a good time to praise our outstanding performance under duress. His failure to mention us left us sore about it. It was all I could do to shake Coach's hand at the celebration ceremony.* Nonetheless, we were state champions in 1961."

Show and Tell

"I was lost, stuck in a phone booth at the corner of Walk and Don't Walk."

- Unknown

The difference between a story and a great story is in the details, as I have mentioned. You should rely on your basic senses – sight, smell, taste, touch and hearing to add those details. You can remember what happened, and if you'll allow yourself to exercise your sensory memory, you'll be able to put together some pieces of the scene by revisiting the scene in your mind. It's there, you just have to go there to get it.

Being placed in the shoes of the main actor, yourself in this case, helps the reader track and vicariously experience what you've experienced. We are more interested in hearing how a handshake felt than just being told you shook hands, in many cases.

Close Your Eyes And Type

I'm not trying to help you become a Pulitzer prize winning writer. If you're not that already, you're going to need a lot of practice and that's another book for you to read. I'm trying to help you tell your story with the skills you already have plus a few tips and how-to's.

Here's how to write something that will capture the imagination of the reader. To do that, you have to describe how things appealed to your own five senses: sight, smell, touch, taste and sound.

You may have a hard time convincing yourself to do this, but I suggest you close your eyes when you're trying to recall or relive a happening in your life. Multi-sensory perception is not as easy as you think it is. You're capable of it, I'm sure. But, did you know that one of the central challenges of the autistic is to employ more than one sense at a time? Some can't hear well when they're seeing at the same time. I can't drive and talk on the phone effectively if the traffic gets serious.

The challenge of the autistic emphasizes the fact that multi-sensory perception is a part of advanced development. But that doesn't mean we can write with both hands simultaneously. And it's difficult to have a conversation while you're trying to write. There are limits to what we can process at one time. You can reduce the challenge of your recall by reducing the challenge on this multi-sensory capability. Close your eyes and focus the energy you have on your inner sense.

We call this your "mind's eye." You can sometimes recall many or most of your senses in a past experience if you try. Close your eyes and recall hugging your grandmother. Can you recall the comfort of her padded arms and the smell of her dentured breath? Or see yourself batting in that semi-final baseball game. Can you recall the smell of the dusty field and the humidity of the day that caused your hands and chest to sweat?

I'm not suggesting you provide the detailed description of a Charles Dickens, but a few sensory details when you first mention a new person, place or thing will bring your reader's "mind's eye" into the story. They, too, will know a grandmother's hug and the dry dust of a field or playground. They'll begin to feel what you felt and empathize with your story.

Consider the difference in the following examples of sensory deprived descriptions and those with the senses employed.

Without visual
"She sat across from me and told me how the affair had happened. It was then the full reality that this was over hit me."

With visual
"She sat across from me *in a folding concert chair underneath the limbs of some large trees in the park. It was an oddly bright and sunny day. It was a day meant for happy things. Her lips tensed and quivered as she told me how the affair had happened. There weren't any tears, though, just the plain facts.* It was then the full reality that this was over hit me."

You might expect that this man's lover would have felt badly as she told him the bad news. But, not necessarily. She might have grimaced as she defiantly spit the news out or she might have sat back and taunted him with the news, her chin held high in air like a dare. The visual description adds meaning to how this terrible moment felt.

Without sound
"I called her over to me from the playground where she and her little friends had been climbing the jungle gym. I asked her what she knew about it. She admitted she had done it."

With sight and sound
"I called her over to me from the playground where she and her little friends had been climbing the jungle gym. I asked her what she knew about it. *She hung her head immediately, her smile turned into a frown, and she whispered in a tiny voice with barely enough breath to finish the sentence,* "I did it.""

This obviously involved a little girl who has found it necessary to confess. She did it without hesitation, to her credit it seems, with a brief, direct admission. She didn't shout it. She whispered it like a little girl who is very sorry. I felt sorry for her.

Without touch
"When the helicopter hit the ground, it exploded. I was lying on the ground somewhere in the jungle in pretty bad shape. I broke my leg badly and I was burned all over. I was there three days before they found me."

With touch
"When the helicopter hit the ground, it exploded. I was lying on the ground somewhere in the jungle in pretty bad shape. I broke my leg badly and I was burned all over. *As I laid there, I felt my whole body to see what was left. I was soaking wet. I didn't understand how at first, but it was blood. When I reached my leg, I felt a sharp, splintered stick in my thigh. That, I figured out in moments, was my leg bone protruding through my trousers.* I was there three days before they found me."

In a scene like this, it is not necessary to carry the description to extremes. But, being "in pretty bad shape" takes on new meaning with just a little description of this horrific event. The surprise of discovering what the wetness was from and the unsuspecting discovery of his broken femur with his hand adds a dimension to the scene that was far too understated in the first version. This is a life altering event and deserves some description so we can capture the gravity of what has happened.

Without smell
"We spent a week at the cabin every summer until my sixteenth birthday. Nobody else ever used this nice cabin in between times, so every year presented considerable cleanup duty. It was a little creepy going in there, but it had to be done."

With smell
"We spent a week at the cabin every summer until my sixteenth birthday. Nobody else ever used this nice cabin in between times, so every year presented considerable

cleanup duty. It was a little creepy going in there, but it had to be done.

After jiggling the lock for quite a long time (it seemed to rust in place every year) we would open the creaking door and step inside. The air in there was as still as a cave's and smelled like the death of a thousand box elder bugs. Whatever it was, it was dead."

Okay, I've been cheating, you've noticed. I've been piling on with sight, sound and the other senses too. It's hard to recollect with only one of your senses and that's all the better.

I can't say I could tell the smell of a thousand dead box elder bugs, but I do have the sense that this cabin was very unused between visits. Somebody else could go in first, as far as I'm concerned.

Without taste

"Mary's first dinner was a surprise in the sense that we neither knew what to expect. We had a hot plate, a toaster, coffee pot, one saucepan and a skillet. She did what she could with her limited resources and experience. It was her first effort and we managed to choke it down."

With taste

"Mary's first dinner was a surprise, in the sense that neither of us knew what to expect. We had a hot plate, a toaster, coffee pot, one saucepan and a skillet. She did what she could with her limited resources and experience. *It didn't taste like anything you'd ever have tasted before, because no one would ever have likely swallowed anything similar. In later years, I once stood in a photographer's dark room and was taken back to that night by the odor in there. That's the best I can do in describing this first meal. We managed to smile at one another* and choke it down."

You have to wonder if this couple got married. Or stayed married. This writer has a wry sense of humor about him, and one can only hope she does too. His description does more than tell about this meal's flavor, of course. It tells about his tolerances and his feelings for Mary at the time – he did manage to smile while he ate this chemical tasting concoction. He was determined to make the best of things, obviously.

Be a camera. Be a microphone. Be a movie director and set the stage for us in every way you can. Place yourself back in time, see yourself in your former wardrobe then see and hear and touch and feel and smell the world as it was then. Don't just tell us what happened, show us.

Questioning Exercises

What can you question?

Challenge: Write as many questions as you can to help this writer flesh out the following selections from stories.

After you've "finished," the first time, you'll find you're not finished. As you read your draft, you will find opportunities to add more details to your story. These exercises give you the opportunity to inspect someone else's writing for opportunities to ask and answer more questions.

As you review your own writing, mark the spots where a question comes to mind. I suggest you mark the spot with a number that corresponds to the question you will write out on a separate sheet of paper. Keep a sheet for each page you mark up and label it with the manuscript's page number. This leaves you lots of room on the paper to easily add more questions to your list without having to squeeze another question in to a tightly packed list.

When are you finished? When you feel you are. There's no rule to follow. I suggest you put your story away for a couple of weeks, or more, and let it breathe before you decide you're truly finished and not just tired. Many an author has let his manuscript sit for a long time, sometimes many years, before pulling it out again to finish it up.

Writing is emotionally taxing. You can get tired. Follow your own instincts and give yourself time to become refreshed between sessions with yourself. When you're done, you'll know you're done.

In what follows you'll see a sample story with a place to write your questions beneath it. When you turn the page, you'll see the same story with footnote markers in the text. That's the point where my questions occurred. Beneath that are the questions I had. They are numbered to correspond to the footnote markers.

Finally, you see a version of the story incorporating some answers to the questions I've posed. From this you can see how a story grows more interesting simply by asking and answering the questions, then incorporating your responses into the text.

Questioning Exercises

Exercise #1

A Trip to Macchu Pichu

When we arrived at Macchu Pichu, there were hundreds of other tourists there waiting to make the ascent. We got off the train and waited our turn to ride the bus to the site of the ruins.

While we waited we were surrounded with several local vendors trying to sell us all kinds of things. I tried to buy some things, but my Spanish was so poor I'm not sure if I overpaid. I got something to eat and spent the waiting period eating. I was thinking I was going to need the energy to climb around those stone structures at the top of the mountain.

When we reached the top, we all piled out of the bus and began meandering the paths around the ruins. We took several photos as we wandered. It was slow going, but it was an afternoon well spent.

Write your questions below.

1.
2.
3.
4.
5.
6.

Questioning Exercises

Exercise #1

A Trip to Macchu Pichu

When we arrived at Macchu Pichu, there were hundreds of other tourists there waiting to make the ascent.[1] We got off the train and waited our turn to ride the bus to the site of the ruins.[2]

While we waited we were surrounded with several local vendors trying to sell us all kinds of things.[3] I tried to buy some things, but my Spanish was so poor I'm not sure if I overpaid.[4] I got something to eat and spent the waiting period eating. I was thinking I was going to need the energy to climb around those stone structures at the top of the mountain.

When we reached the top, we all piled out of the bus and began meandering the paths around the ruins.[5] We took several photos as we wandered. It was slow going, but it was an afternoon well spent.[6]

My Questions…

1. What did it look like at the place you arrived to wait for the bus?

2. What did the train look like and how was the ride there?

3. What were they selling? How did they approach you?

4. How did you try to communicate with the vendors? What did you buy? How did you feel trying to do business using a language you barely knew?

5. What did you see when you first got off? What was the ride to the top like?

6. Why was it "slow going?"

Exercise #1
A Trip to Macchu Pichu

We got off the train and waited our turn to ride the bus to the site of the ruins. It was a long train ride aboard cars that more resembled streetcars than typical train cars. The windows were wide and tall. From any seat I could watch the wildly turbulent Orinoco River run parallel to the tracks all the way there. The river water boiled volcanically and ran as fast as a waterfall.

When we arrived at Macchu Pichu, there were hundreds of other tourists there waiting to make the ascent. The small town at the base of the camp was a dusty assembly of tin and canvas, open-air shops. The streets were full of tourists browsing one shop after the next.

While we waited we were surrounded with several local vendors trying to sell us all kinds of things. Women, men and children confronted all of us in packs. They held up all kinds of items, ponchos, hats, jewelry, postcards and food. I tried to buy some things, but my Spanish was so poor I'm not sure if I overpaid. They were eager to sell and did their best to understand my sign language and bits of Spanish I offered to explain myself. It was pleasing to see I could get along with limited Spanish that way.

I got something to eat and spent the waiting period eating. I got what looked like an ear of corn with the largest kernels I've ever seen. They called it "choclo." It was steamed cooked and served with a white cheese that was delicious and filling. I was thinking I was going to need the energy to climb around those stone structures at the top of the mountain. After my snack, I could have climbed all day.

When we reached the top, we all piled out of the bus and began meandering the paths around the ruins. The ruins were made of large stones, each stone being several feet wide and high. The structures were laid out in geometric patterns on various plateaus in this small community.

We took several photos as we wandered. It was slow going, but it was an afternoon well spent. Macchu Pichu is located 11,000 feet high in the mountains and the air is thin. I huffed and puffed and had to sit every few minutes for the lack of oxygen.

Comments

The writer could have expanded this story further with more description and emotional responses to the experience. How far you take the story depends on the value you assign to the story. You may agree, though, that the few details that were added make this tale come alive compared to the original version.

My Questions…

1. What did it look like at the place you arrived to wait for the bus?
   There was a small, dusty town there full of shops.

2. What did the train look like and how was the ride there?
   It was a scenic ride along a great river.

3. What were they selling? How did they approach you?
   They sold a variety of goods including some impressive corn.

4. How did you try to communicate with the vendors? What did you buy? How did you feel trying to do business using a language you barely knew?
   It was satisfying to be able to accomplish the purchase using sign language and what Spanish he had.

Questioning Exercises

5. What did you see when you first got off? What was the ride like to the top?
   There were the great stone structures laid out on plateaus in a geometric pattern.

6. Why was it "slow going?"
   He suffered from lack of oxygen being so far up in the mountains.

Exercise #2

My First Army Reserve Camp

I rode to camp in the back of an Army truck. It was a boring, long ride to Ft. McCoy. We were to spend two weeks there practicing our trade, the artillery. I don't recommend traveling this way to anybody.

We got our duffle bags and went to our barracks. There's nothing comfortable about them either. Everyday we would get up and go out to the field to practice shooting at targets. This lasted until the late afternoon when we made our way back to the base.

I wasn't a particularly enthusiastic soldier, but I did a reasonable job when called upon to do my part in the exercises. I'm not so sure, though, that we would have stood the test of real battle based on what we accomplished there.

Write your questions below.

1. _____

2. _____

3. _____

4. _____

5. _____

6. _____

Exercise #2

My First Army Reserve Camp

I rode to camp in the back of an Army truck.[1] It was a boring, long ride to Ft. McCoy.[2] We were to spend two weeks there practicing our trade, the artillery.[3] I don't recommend traveling this way to anybody.

We got our duffle bags and went to our barracks. There's nothing comfortable about them either.[4] Everyday we would get up and go out to the field to practice shooting at targets.[5] This lasted until the late afternoon when we made our way back to the base.

I wasn't a particularly enthusiastic soldier,[6] but I did a reasonable job when called upon to do my part in the exercises.[7] I'm not so sure, though, that we would have stood the test of real battle based on what we accomplished there.

My Questions…

1. What kind of a truck was it and how did you ride in the back?
2. How did you handle the boredom?
3. What artillery did your unit shoot? And where is Ft. McCoy?
4. What were the barracks like?
5. How did you practice shooting? How did it go?
6. How and why weren't you an "enthusiastic soldier?"
7. What was your job in the army?

Exercise #2

My First Army Reserve Camp

I rode to camp in the back of a "deuce and a quarter" Army truck, that is, a two and half ton truck. I sat on one of the two wooden pull-down benches used to transport troops when it was not hauling supplies. It was a pounding ride and prevented any napping because of the constant jolting. I was hammered this way for six and half hours.

It was a boring ride to Ft. McCoy, a sprawling camp located in central southern Wisconsin. Some friends and I tried to pass the time any way we could to distract ourselves. We ogled the passengers of passing cars, told tales of past camp experiences and, thanks to a recent interest of mine, we challenged each other to memory contests. I would have someone recite a series of words, nouns, and bet the contributor that I could recite the list back to him in a show of my powerful memory. I could instantly memorize and recite a list of around a hundred words. I made a couple of bucks, but earned more value from the challenge in creating a reputation. I don't recommend traveling this way to anybody.

We were to spend two weeks there practicing our trade, shooting the eight-inch howitzer. This gun looked something like a tank. The huge howitzer was mounted on a vehicle that traveled on tracks and could shoot a two-hundred pound shell twenty miles. I was amazed we were trusted to commit such an act.

We got our duffle bags and went to our barracks. There's nothing comfortable about them either. The Army must have purchased all there was of this special kind of beige they paint these barracks with. Nothing could look so cold and uninviting as barracks beige. Inside the floors were a dark, dead brown linoleum that even buffed up looked like dirt. Rows of metal bunk beds lined each half of the floor. This was home for two weeks.

Everyday we would get up and go out to the field to practice shooting at targets. After a breakfast of watery eggs, petrified bacon and dry biscuits, they sent us to the field to fire the howitzers. A breakfast like that brought out the killer in us and made the prospect of even feigned violence appealing. Once well out into the hinterland, some unseen soldier miles out front would tell us where to aim. We would load a shell and a bag of black powder behind it, fire it off and wait for the results. We were never told if we hit anything, but given the permission to fire again we figured we hadn't done anything too wrong. So we'd shoot again. This lasted until the late afternoon when we made our way back to the base.

I wasn't a particularly enthusiastic soldier. My term of service was during the Viet Nam war and this battalion of soldiers was made up of government sanctioned draft dodgers. We didn't believe in the war, so we went through these motions as payment for our excused absence from the front line jungle in Viet Nam.

I did a reasonable job when called upon to do my part in the exercises. I was a gunner, that is, I sat beside the mammoth barrel on the howitzer and aimed it. We were once awarded the honor of "Best Battery." I guess I hit something. I'm not so sure, though, that we would have stood the test of real battle based on what we accomplished there.

Comments

Notice how adding physical details has brought out feelings about his experience. Overall, we get the feeling that the value of the whole summer camp experience was doubtful from his perspective. All of these aspects come together to present a multi-dimensional illustration of this time in his life.

1. What kind of a truck was it and how did you ride in the back?
   The detail (a "deuce and a quarter") adds color to the story and provoked his recollection of how uncomfortable the trip was. He felt "hammered."

2. How did you handle the boredom?
   An interesting piece of the story was triggered when telling about dealing with boredom. His memory game was different and his reward for it was not just money, it was reputation. He liked that, apparently.

3. What artillery did your unit shoot? And where is Ft. McCoy?
   It is necessary to set the stage with at least the minimum of information. Tell the reader where you are.

4. What were the barracks like?
   The barracks were "cold and uninviting" he tells us. He paints the atmosphere for his unrewarding time there in framing the living quarters this way.

5. How did you practice shooting? How did it go?
   He casts a great deal of doubt on the value of the training. He was unimpressed.

6. How and why weren't you an "enthusiastic soldier?"
   He didn't support the war like all others there. This tells the

reader something important about the times in which he is living.

7. What was your job in the army?
   He was a gunner. This is another of those stage-setting details that answers an obvious question. What was he doing there?

Exercise #3

Getting Married the Second Time

So here I was doing it again. I got married in a small church in a town I had never been in before. Maybe that should have told me something. There were a hundred or so people there and the ceremony came off without a hitch.

We left the church in the usual manner and got in my car to take off for the honeymoon. We didn't have much money, so our honeymoon was nothing more than an overnight in an expensive hotel. The food was good.

After that, we went home to the apartment we'd been sharing in Peoria. We went back to work the next day.

Write your questions below.

1. _____

2. _____

3. _____

4. _____

5. _____

6. _____

Questioning Exercises

Exercise #3

Getting Married the Second Time

So here I was doing it again. I got married in a small church in a town I had never been in before.[1] Maybe that should have told me something.[2] There were a hundred or so people there and the ceremony came off without a hitch.[3]

We left the church in the usual manner and got in my car to take off for the honeymoon.[4] We didn't have much money, so our honeymoon was nothing more than an overnight in an expensive hotel.[5] The food was good.

After that, we went home to the apartment we'd been sharing in Peoria.[6] We went back to work the next day.

My Questions...

1. Why were you getting married in a strange town?
2. What should that have told you?
3. Who was at the wedding?
4. What is the "usual manner" of leaving a church wedding?
5. Where did you go and what was it like?
6. Why and how long had you been sharing an apartment?

Exercise #3

Getting Married the Second Time

So here I was doing it again. I got married in a small church in a town I had never been in before. The church was her choice. I had and have no religion. So I was married in a church that I hadn't seen before, in a town I never knew before and by a minister I had met only once. Maybe that should have told me something – like how little I knew about what I was doing and who I was marrying.

There were a hundred or so people there and the ceremony came off without a hitch, with the exception of the marriage itself. Of the hundred guests that were there, I knew probably less than one in four. I cared no more about them than they could have cared about me. Such is the way of wedding ceremonies, it seems. It's so much flourish and so little substance.

We left the church in the usual manner. I took off for the honeymoon, this time in a different car than the last, with a different wife but, tragically in the same marriage. It was doomed.

We didn't have much money, so our honeymoon was nothing more than an overnight in an expensive hotel. We spent the night in the Hyatt Regency eating fine food, drinking champagne and later watching TV. The food was good.

After that, we went home to the apartment we'd been sharing in Peoria. We'd spent a year together in the apartment while we both worked in the same electronics store. Our common interest was the business and everyone needs a place to stay. We went back to work the next day.

Questioning Exercises

Comments

This version of events tells us a lot more about this second marriage. We have a hint with the wistful opening line. But it begs for explanation and we get it when the questions are answered.

1. Why were you getting married in a strange town?
   It was her choice and he was not involved.

2. What should "that have told you?"
   It told him that he did not really know what he was getting into.

3. Who was at the wedding?
   He felt surrounded by strangers. It was assembly without connection or meaning to him.

4. What is the "usual manner" of leaving a church wedding?
   He now feels the marriage was an unfortunate replay of his last failed marriage.

5. Where did you go and what was it like?
   It was not a romantic flight.

6. Why and how long had you been sharing an apartment?
   Their relationship lacked depth and seemed more a matter of convenience.

Design And Layout

"One of the great deceptions in life is when you're down to the last 5% of the job, you're only half done."

- David Eubanks

Where you put what you have is the challenge of page design and layout. There are a handful of software programs you might use to write your story. Desktop publishing programs like Adobe's FrameMaker and PageMaker, QuarkXpress and Microsoft's Publisher are all programs you might use if you own one of them. However, the most common program used today is Microsoft Word. It's not actually a desktop publishing program, but it acts like one in many respects. Most importantly, you can insert photographs in your text about any way you want to, although it can be a little unruly in the process. You can accomplish about anything you want to using Word.

You can create a single or double column layout with ease. This discussion will focus on a single column layout with wide margins. You may agree that this provides a sophisticated look befitting a keepsake volume such as the one you're about to create. Take a look at the sample layouts on the following pages.

Design And Layout

A Standard Layout
A standard layout may look like the sample pages below.

> by corn and soybean fields, flat fields of crops stretching as far as the eye could see. And lots of people made their living from the fruits of those fields.
>
> **Places I've Lived**
> I have a very faint recollection of living on Lincoln Street in Decatur, my first home. I know that we lived there until I was about three years old and then we moved briefly, for a summer, to a house on Vanderhoof. Then we moved to the first home I can remember well. That was 273 Columbus Drive located in a new subdivision on the north side of Decatur.
>
> I was about three and half and I remember moving in to the house on Columbus. There was no grass in our lawn or in any of the lawns nearby. It appeared to have been built in a recently plowed cornfield with large dirt clods everywhere. The week we moved in, my father went out in the backyard and found a huge dead rat. He went out and picked it up by the tail and put it in a Tide box and left it sitting in the driveway near the garbage can. I spent a week riding my tricycle by that rat and keeping an eye on it. I remember the rat tail sticking out of that box and what an ugly, frightening scene that was. Then it went away, but I still remember the rat.
>
> The house was a three bedroom ranch, very typical of the 1950's style. It had a hip roof, a small yellow brick planter in the front which my mother planted with petunias of the purple and multi-colored variety. I used to ride my trike along those petunias. I've always loved petunias ever since. I think it was the kind of house that would have been the epitome of 1950's success.
>
> 5

This page uses two-inch margins, extra spacing between paragraphs and ample interline spacing to give the text an airy feel. It looks good and makes for easier reading too.

Design And Layout

Standard Picture Layout
This page shows pictures positioned on a separate page apart

from the narrative text. Notice the pictures are captioned.

Design And Layout

showed up and sang into one microphone just the way the Everly Brothers did, and learned how to lean just the right way towards the mike so both our voices would be heard. We got a lot of praise and reward for doing this. Over the next couple of years, 6th, 7th, and 8th grade, we gave lots of performances and got at some little breaks.

The Illinois State Fair

Once we sang at the Illinois State Fair. It was there we met a local group called the Sangamon Valley Boys, a country band with the typical country

instrumentation: lead guitar, acoustic guitar, stand up electric bass, steel guitar, drums and some lead singers. They were local heroes. They had their own TV show called Cornbelt Country Style hosted by Uncle Johnny Barton. We really admired these guys. We had once before seen them play the opening of a car dealership. They set up in the showroom and a crowd of fifty or seventy-five people watched them play and I'll say that it was one of the best live

Custom Layouts

Here the photograph is positioned with the text appearing either above or below the text. Placing a picture adjacent to the related text makes the reading easier and more interesting.

Design And Layout

Custom Layout (continued)
For a fancier look, have the text wrap around all sides of the text.

showed up and sang into one microphone just the way the Everly Brothers did, and learned how to lean just the right way towards the mike so both our voices would be heard. We got a lot of praise and reward for doing this. Over the next couple of years, 6th, 7th, and 8th grade, we gave lots of performances and got at some little breaks.

The Illinois State Fair

Once we sang at the Illinois State Fair. It was there we met a local group called the Sangamon Valley Boys, a country band with the typical country instrumentation: lead guitar, acoustic guitar, stand up electric bass, steel guitar, drums and some lead singers. They were local heroes. They had their own TV show called Cornbelt Country Style hosted by Uncle Johnny Barton. We really admired these guys. We had once before seen them play the opening of a car dealership. They set up in the

showroom and a crowd of fifty or seventy-five people watched them play and I'll say that it was one of the best live performances I've ever seen. It's surprising how the great performances you see are often unexpected and that was unexpected. Junior Garner, the lead singer, had an absolutely first rate beautiful voice, and Uncle Johnny Barton was a pro as an emcee. John's mother sang country music and we had become very familiar with a lot of country songs by the big stars like Hank Williams, Jim Reeves, and Patsy Cline. We knew all

5

Design And Layout

To achieve the elegant look of a keepsake book, as opposed to the wall-to-wall text seen in a paperback novel, I suggest large margins all around. Set up your document for "mirror margins" so the program can automatically allow for a little extra space for the binding on the inside margins. Try the following page setup using the standard 8 ½ x 11 letter-sized page.

Note: The commands you will see in some of the following instructions will ask you to choose a menu and menu items. An example of the syntax of those commands is this:

File>Save As

This means click on the **File** menu, then choose the **Save As** item on the menu.

Design And Layout

Setting Up the Page in Microsoft Word

Step	Result
1. Choose **File>Page Setup**.	The Page Setup dialog box appears.

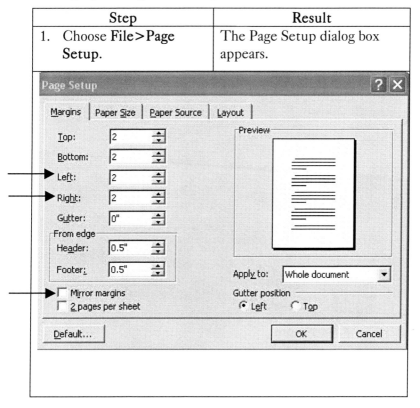

Design And Layout

2. Check the *Mirror Margins* check box.	The *Right* and *Left* labels change to *Inside* and *Outside*.

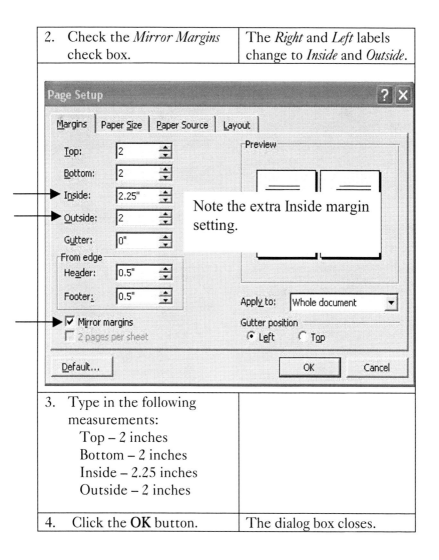

Note the extra Inside margin setting.

3. Type in the following measurements:
    Top – 2 inches
    Bottom – 2 inches
    Inside – 2.25 inches
    Outside – 2 inches	

4. Click the **OK** button.	The dialog box closes.

Design And Layout

Tip: Word allows you to use up to 256 characters in your file name, including spaces. Name your files intuitively, so the contents are suggested by the name. This will make arranging the sequence of your files easier when you finally compile them all.

I think it's convenient for each file to have a consistent and finished look as you create them. Therefore, I suggest you make a template of the file using the margins you just set. Each time you begin a new file, you will use the template to create the file and it will automatically have the identical margins. Here's how:

Making a Template

Step	Result
1. Choose **File>Save As**.	The *Save As* dialog box appears.

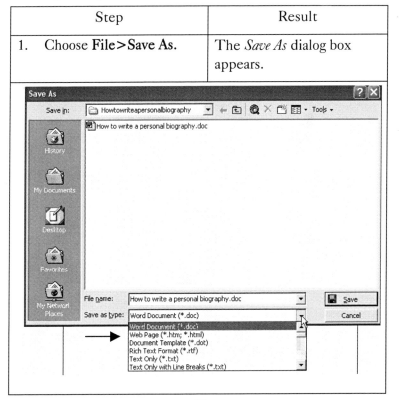

Design And Layout

2. Click the *Save as type:* drop down arrow and **choose** *Document Template* from the list.	The *Save in:* folder becomes the *Template* folder.
3. Type the name **My Bio** in the *Filename:* box.	The file will automatically take on the ".dot" extension.
4. Click the **Save** button.	The dialog box closes.
KEEP THE FILE OPEN FOR THE NEXT STEPS.	

You'll want your text to have an elegant look to it too. "White space" such as the space provided around the edges of the text on the page creates an elegant look. Added inter-paragraph spacing and line spacing is also recommended to add to the special look.

You will modify some of the paragraph styles provided by Word to achieve this. Paragraph styles can be applied to one or more paragraphs at a time. Once applied, the paragraph immediately takes on all the formatting as defined by the style. For example, the paragraph will appear with the specific font you've chosen, use the before and after paragraph spacing, and use the chosen line spacing.

I'll show you how to modify one paragraph style. Once you can modify one style and add it to your template, you can modify any others you wish to modify using the same steps.

Design And Layout

Adding Modified Paragraph Styles to Your Template

Step	Result
1. Choose **Format>Style**.	The *Style* dialog box appears.
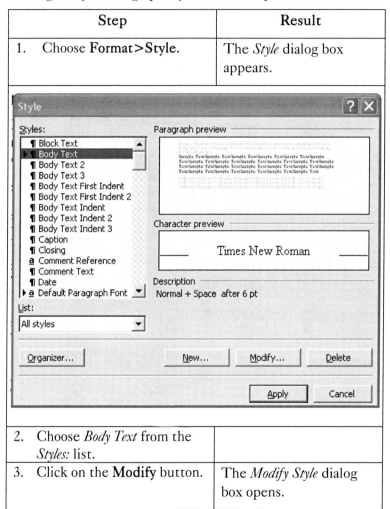	
2. Choose *Body Text* from the *Styles:* list.	
3. Click on the **Modify** button.	The *Modify Style* dialog box opens.

Design And Layout

Adding Modified Paragraph Styles to Your Template

Step	Result
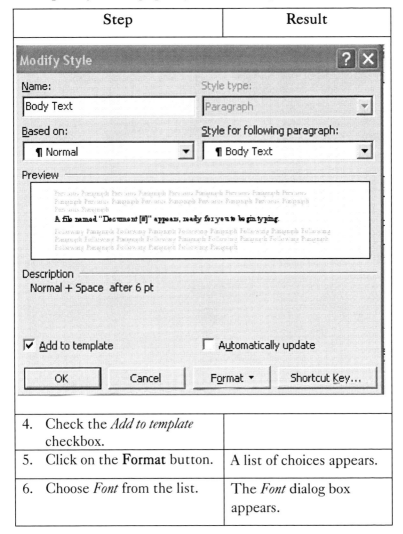	
4. Check the *Add to template* checkbox.	
5. Click on the **Format** button.	A list of choices appears.
6. Choose *Font* from the list.	The *Font* dialog box appears.

Design And Layout

Adding Modified Paragraph Styles to Your Template

Step	Result
[Font dialog box screenshot showing Font tab selected, with Font: Times New Roman, Font style: Regular, Size: 12, Font color: Automatic, Underline style: (none), and various Effects checkboxes. Preview shows "Times New Roman".]	
7. Choose a font from the font list.	
Tip: Choose a serif font like the one you're seeing in this text as opposed to a sans serif font like this: sample. Serif fonts are generally easier to read and look more sophisticated.	
8. Choose an 11 point size from the font size list.	

Design And Layout

Adding Modified Paragraph Styles to Your Template

Step	Result
1. Click on the **OK** button.	The dialog box closes.
2. Click the **Modify** button again.	The *Modify Style* dialog box opens.
3. Click on the *Format* button again.	A list of choices appears.
4. Choose *Paragraph* from the list.	The *Paragraph* dialog box appears.

Design And Layout

Adding Modified Paragraph Styles to Your Template

Step	Result
1. Make the following changes: Change the *After:* setting to *6 pt*. Change the *Line Spacing:* settings to *Exactly* and *14 pt*.	
2. Click the **OK** buttons until all the dialog boxes are closed.	
3. Choose **File > Save As**.	The *Save As* dialog box appears.
4. Choose *Document* Template from the *Save as type:* drop down list.	
5. Click on the *My Bio* icon in the list of templates.	
6. Click on the **Save** button.	The dialog box closes and you have updated your template with this change to the Body Text paragraph style.

You may want to modify the Heading 1, Heading 2 and Heading 3 paragraph styles too. For example, you may want to change the font and size to coordinate with your Body Text font and size. I suggest you use the same font face for headings and body text. You may choose to use something different for chapter titles, using the Heading 1 style, for example, but it is recommended to use not more than two or three font faces in a single document. The document can begin to look like a ransom note if too many fonts appear.

Here are my suggestions for the font settings in your Headings styles:

Style	Size	Format	Purpose
Heading 1	18 pt	Bold	Chapter Titles
Heading 2	14 pt	Bold	Section Headings
Heading 3	12 pt	Italic	Section sub-headings

Three levels of headings should be enough to guide the reader through your story. Here are some examples of Chapter Titles, Section and Section sub-headings you might use.

Heading Style	Type of Heading	Sample Subjects	Purpose
Heading 1	Chapter Titles	Early Childhood Occupations Education	Broad topics
Heading 2	Section Headings	My Homes Welder North Central College	More focused subjects

Design And Layout

Heading Style	Type of Heading	Sample Subjects	Purpose
Heading 3	Section sub-headings	Measles and Mumps Getting Promoted Changing Majors	Episodes and events

Now that you've created a template, here's how you can use it to create a new file.

Using the Template to Create a New File

Step	Result
1. Choose **File<New**.	The *New* dialog box appears.

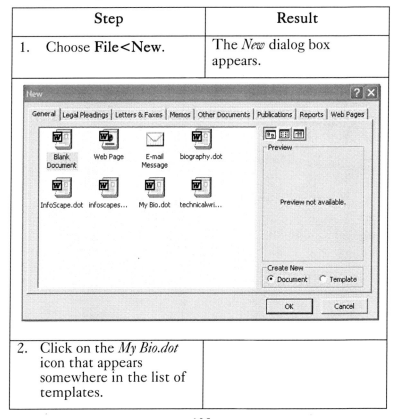

2. Click on the *My Bio.dot* icon that appears somewhere in the list of templates.	

105

Design And Layout

3. Click on the **OK** button.	A file named *Document* [#] appears, ready for you to begin typing.
4. Save the file using an intuitive filename as previously suggested.	

You will probably create a number of files. Here's how to keep the files organized so when you assemble the entire book, you'll know better where on your computer to look to find the files you want.

You should create one master folder that will hold all your files. Within the master folder you should create a number of folders named after the categories I mentioned in the beginning of this book. Once again, they are:

- Childhood
- Children
- Education
- Family of Origin
- Family
- Friends
- Fun
- Marriage
- Work
- Retirement
- Service
- Special Subjects: Creativity, Avocations, Medical

Design And Layout

How to Create a Master Folder

Creating a Folder

Step	Result
1. Point to the **Start** button and right-click. (Click the right button on your mouse.)	A menu of choices appears.
2. Choose *Explore* from the menu.	The Windows Explorer panel appears.
3. Click on the *Local Disk (C:)* icon.	The icon and name is highlighted.
4. Choose **File>New>Folder**.	A new folder appears with the name *New Folder* highlighted.
5. Type "My Bio."	*New Folder* is replaced.

Design And Layout

Here's how to make sub-folders in the master folder:

Creating Sub-folders

Step	Result
1. Double-click the "My Bio" folder in the list of folders and files.	A blank area appears to the right of the folders list.
2. Right-click in the blank area.	A menu of choices appears.
3. Choose **File>New>Folder**.	A folder appears named *New Folder* as before.
4. Type the name of the folder using the suggested categories listed at the beginning of this section and press the [**Enter**] key.	
5. Repeat the process until you have created the desired number of folders.	

Now that you've created the necessary folders, you may save your files into any of those folders. Here's how to save a file into a particular folder:

Design And Layout

Saving a File to a Selected Folder

Step	Result
1. Choose **File>Save As**.	The *Save As* dialog box opens.
2. Click the *Save in:* drop down arrow.	The drives and folders list appears.
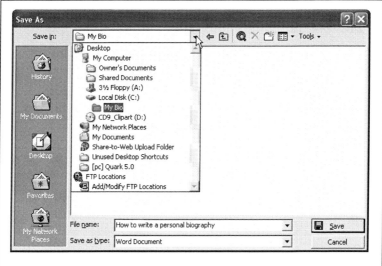	
3. Click on the C: drive icon, then click the *My Bio* folder.	The *My Bio* folder appears in the *Save in:* text box, and the subfolders appear in the list below.
4. Click on the subfolder into which you want to save the file.	The subfolder opens showing any files that may be already stored there.
5. Click the **Save** button.	The file is saved into the folder.

Design And Layout

Compiling the Files into One File

I suggest you write your story in small segments. If you are inspired to write about the time you had those harrowing experiences at Boy Scout camp, write and save that in a file. When you want to write another experience, write and save that in another file.

When you've written all you intend to write, you will put all the files into a single file. This is a fairly simple process. Here's how:

Inserting Files

Step	Results
1. Choose **File>New**.	The *New* dialog box appears.
2. Click on the *My Bio.dot* icon.	
3. Click on the **OK** button.	A blank page appears using the settings from the *My Bio* template.
4. Type in the title you wish.	
5. Choose **Insert>File...**	The *Insert File* dialog box appears.

```
Insert File                                                    ? X
Look in:  [ My Bio                    ]  ← ↑  Q × ☐ ▦ ▾ Tools ▾
          Children
          Family
 History  Family of Origin
          Fun
          Special Activities
          Work
 My Documents
```

Design And Layout

Step	Results
6. Choose the *My Bio* folder from the *Look in:* drop down list.	The subfolders are displayed in the folders and files list.
7. Double-click the folder that holds the first file of the book.	The files in the chosen folder are displayed.
8. Double-click on the file you want to insert.	

Tip: Use the file preview feature in the *Insert File* dialog box to be sure you're inserting the correct file. You can scroll through the file's text with this feature before inserting the file.

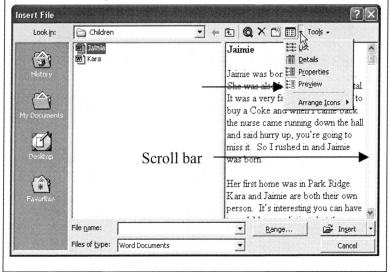

Design And Layout

Step	Results
9. Position your insertion point on a blank line beneath the inserted file and repeat the process above until all files have been inserted.	

Including Photographs

You may write a text only document, but many would like to include some photos. You won't put in as many photos as you would in a photo album, of course, but choosing what to put in can be puzzling. Here are some suggestions of what you might include:

- A picture portrait of each of your children as an adult (option: include a younger photo)
- A picture portrait of each of you and your spouse
- A wedding photo
- A picture portrait photo as individuals or couples of your parents and in-laws
- A picture portrait or family photo of you and your siblings
- Special event photos - graduations, celebrations, special travel
- A photo of your various homes' exterior
- Any photo of very special importance

You might also consider including special documents.

- Special letters, for example, from the war years or a last letter
- Historical documents of interest – passports, wills, posters, deeds, discharge papers, special deeds
- News articles
- Personal publications – a special letter or cover page from a published article

Here's how you place a photograph in your text and have the text wrap around it using Microsoft Word:

How to Include a Photograph in Text

Inserting a Photograph

Step	Result
1. Place your insertion point at the place in the text where you want the picture to appear.	
Note: The picture will appear with the wrapping style *In line with text* automatically. You may choose a different wrapping style and move the picture later.	
2. Choose **Insert>Picture> From file ...**	The *Insert Picture* dialog box appears.
3. Click on the folder icon that holds the picture.	
4. Click on the picture's filename.	
5. Click on the **Insert** button.	The picture appears in

Design And Layout

Inserting a Photograph

Step	Result
	the text.
 We live in a time when there has been a displacement of family continuity and vales by a stream of media-produced banality. Vulgar and shallow. Bereft of meaning. Void of the values of personal relationship in any dimension. We are in an age when today's children may know more about Madonna's personal ← *In line with text wrapping with picture selected showing sizing handles* history than their own grandparents, and perhaps parents, too. Preserving a piece of family history in a book creates a priceless family heirloom that gains in value with every passing year. I think it's one of the best things anyone could do for the family.	
6. With the picture still selected, you may resize the picture by dragging one of the corner handles (the black squares) towards or away from the center of the photo.	
7. Point to the photo and right-click.	The *Format Picture* dialog box appears.
8. Click on the *Layout* tab.	The layout options appear.

Design And Layout

Inserting a Photograph

Step	Result
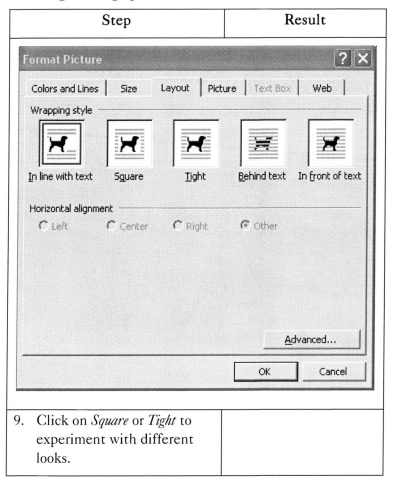	
9. Click on *Square* or *Tight* to experiment with different looks.	

Inserting a Photograph

Step	Result
10. Drag the picture to the desired location.	
Picture With *Square* Wrapping Setting and in a New Location We live in a time when there has been a displacement of family continuity and vales by a stream of media-produced banality. Vulgar and shallow. Bereft of meaning. Void of the values of personal relationship in any dimension. We are in an age when today's children may know more about Madonna's personal history than their own grandparents, and perhaps parents, too. Preserving a piece of family history in a book creates a priceless family heirloom that gains in value with every passing year. I think it's one of the best things anyone could do for the family. We need to know something about our pasts, our roots in order to know something about ourselves. The famous Russell Baker, NY Times columnist wrote that, "...our children have the right to know from whence they came." So they know the stuff from which they are made.	
Tip: Click on the **Advanced** button to access the *Top and Bottom* option that will place text above and below the photo but not next to either side of the photo.	
11. Click the **OK** button.	The dialog box closes.

Your book will be easier to understand and read if you caption your photographs. Unfortunately, the caption feature in Word insists on numbering the caption. That's nice for a technical document, but isn't suitable for what you're doing.

Design And Layout

You will have to add a caption using the Text Box tool on the Drawing toolbar. You will group the picture and caption so you can position them as a single unit. Here's how you do it:

Adding a Caption to a Picture

Step	Result
1. Choose **View>Toolbars**, then select *Drawing* from the list.	The Drawing toolbar is displayed (at the bottom of your screen).
Text Box tool	
2. Click on the *Text Box* tool.	The cursor becomes a crosshair when you roll it into the document window.
3. Drag a rectangular shape beneath the picture. (Resize the box as necessary using the square sizing handles.)	A blinking insertion point appears within the box.
4. Type the caption name.	
5. Drag through the letters and use the Format toolbar to choose a font and size you want.	
6. Right-click on the dotted edge of the text box.	The *Format Text Box* opens up.

Design And Layout

Adding a Caption to a Picture

Step	Result
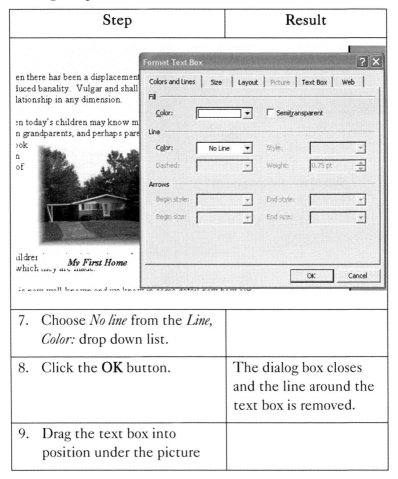	
7. Choose *No line* from the *Line, Color:* drop down list.	
8. Click the **OK** button.	The dialog box closes and the line around the text box is removed.
9. Drag the text box into position under the picture	

Design And Layout

Step	Result
10. If needed, click on the text box to select it (the sizing handles will display), then hold the **Shift** key and click on the picture	Sizing handles appear around both the picture and the text box.
11. Click on the **Draw** button on the left end of the Drawing toolbar.	A menu of choices pops up.
12. Click on the *Group* item at the top of the list.	Sizing handles surround the picture and text box as a single object.

You can position the grouped items as a single unit and apply a wrapping style to the group. If you need to make an adjustment to the caption or picture, you can ungroup them by clicking on the **Draw** button on the Drawing toolbar. An *Ungroup* choice will appear on the list.

Pagination

You may want to separate your story in to chapters. If you do, you will want the first page of a chapter to appear as a right-facing page. That is, when you open to the first page of the chapter, it begins on the right hand page.

You can preview the pagination using the preview command in Word. There you will be able to see where you need to insert blank pages to force the chapter beginning onto the right-facing page. Here's how you do it:

Design And Layout

Previewing Pagination

Step	Result
1. Click on the **Print Preview** icon on the Standard toolbar.	
Print Preview icon.	
2. Choose the two-page view by clicking on the *Multiple Pages* icon and dragging through the first two page icons in the drop down palette.	Two pages from your document appear side by side on screen.
3. Press **Page Up** or **Page Down** to see other pages.	
4. Click on any page once to zoom in, click again to zoom out.	

Design And Layout

Previewing Pagination

Step	Result
Note which pages need to be moved to right-facing pages. Page numbers show on the status bar at the bottom of your screen.	
5. Click the **Close** button on the preview toolbar when finished.	You return to the previous view of the document.

Now you're ready to move the section beginning to the right-facing pages.

Inserting Page Breaks

Step	Result
1. Place your insertion point before the first character on the page that needs to be moved.	
2. Press the key combination **Ctrl + Enter**.	A manual page break is inserted and the page content moves to the following page.
Note: To remove a page break, click the **Show/Hide** button ¶ to reveal the non-printing symbols. Click on the manual page break symbol and press the **Delete** key to remove it.	

know·the·stuff·from·which·they·are·made.¶
¶
⋯⋯⋯⋯⋯⋯⋯⋯⋯⋯⋯⋯⋯⋯⋯⋯Page Break⋯⋯⋯⋯⋯⋯⋯⋯⋯⋯⋯⋯⋯⋯⋯⋯

Design And Layout

Inserting page numbers

Step	Result
1. Place your insertion point anywhere in the document.	
2. Choose **Insert>Page Number**.	The *Page Numbers* dialog box opens.
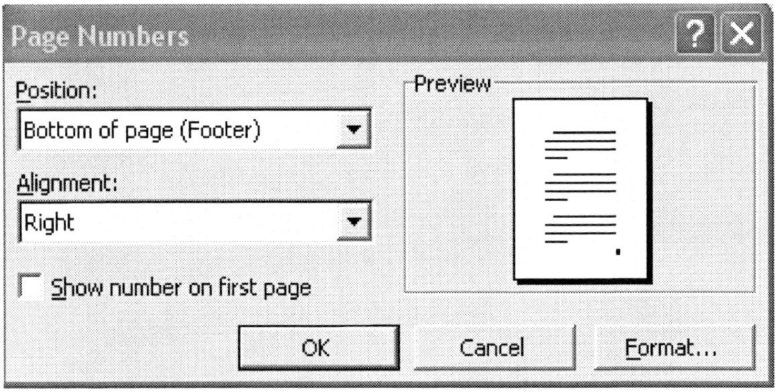 *[Page Numbers dialog box screenshot: Position: Bottom of page (Footer); Alignment: Right; Show number on first page unchecked; OK, Cancel, Format... buttons; Preview pane]*	
3. Choose where you want the page number to appear in the footer at the bottom of the page (right, center, or left) from the *Alignment* drop down list.	Adds number to the bottom of all pages in the document.
4. Clear the check mark, if necessary, from the *Show number on first page* check box.	Prevents the page number from appearing on the first page in the document.

Scanning and Photoediting

There's a great deal to photoediting if you're doing it professionally. As I've said before, this book of for the rest of us who are just trying to get this one thing done – writing our personal biography. I'm going to give you the brief version of what you can do with the photographs you may put in your book.

You really can't improve much on a blurry picture. You can do something about brightness and contrast so it doesn't look so washed out or quite so dark. You can change it from color to black and white. And you can resize it.

I suggest you scan your photographs with the grayscale photograph setting at 600 dpi. Check your scanning software program's options and settings. They're usually obviously available on the screen. If you scan a color photo with the grayscale/ black and white setting, the file size is smaller and may speed the printing process a bit later. You scan at 600 dpi because I recommend that you print to a printer that has a minimum of 600 dpi capability to get a typeset look to your pages. 300 dpi is not really satisfactory.

I suggest you scan the photographs into the TIF format. JPG is popular now because it's used to post pictures to the web in a smaller file size. It's fine for printing too, but if you use JPG in a photoediting program, make changes in a photo and re-save it, the photo loses some of its detail each time you save it. TIF is a larger format in file size, but in grayscale images this is not a big deal.

I've already shown you how to insert pictures into your text. Now's here's a little bit on modifying the photo. When your photograph is selected, Word automatically pops up the **Picture** Toolbar.

Design And Layout

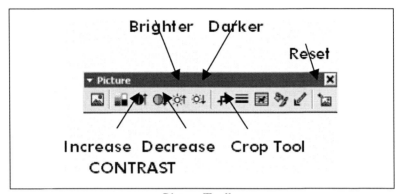

Picture Toolbar

Click on either contrast button to experiment with its effects. You can do the same with the brighter and darker buttons.

The crop tool works a little differently. Click once on the crop tool then drag any one of the sizing handles towards the center of the picture to eliminate part of the photo from visibility. When you're done, click the crop tool again to return to the standard editing mode.

If you don't like the changes you've made, click the reset button on the right end of the toolbar to return the picture to its initial state.

Transcribing Techniques

There are two ways to go about writing your story. You can sit at the keyboard and type it out. Or you could record yourself with a cassette recorder and have the text transcribed later.

If you've never seen the transcribed oral testimony of an individual, you're in for surprise. It's amazing how unlike the written word we speak. We false start, repeat, skip and change subjects with abandon. Many of those whose interviews I transcribed have found themselves aghast at their manner of speaking when seeing the words in print. That's simply due to the nature of spontaneous thought and speech. But it's easier than typing for many.

The difficulty lies in editing the transcribed word into printable form. That's a great deal of work. If you can do this well, you may as well type it in the first place. But, if you're not a typist, here's another idea.

I have employed a method of "re-recording" an oral history that clients have recorded in our initial interviews. I use two tape recorders. I play the original tape on one. On the other, I record the edited version of their thoughts. In this way, I can capture much of their "voice," their sayings and manner of speaking while I am also straightening out the mangled words of spontaneous speech.

I can take the "re-recorded" tapes to a transcription service and have a nearly finished draft of the text made from those tapes. There's always some editing and reorganizing to do, but much of the false starts, redundancy, "so's", "oh, well's" and such can be removed in the process.

Quick Reference

Setting the Stage

- What happened?
- Where did it happen?
- When did it happen?
- Who did what?

Describing Persons, Places or Things

- Tell three things about the person, place or thing when you introduce it in the story.
- If you can, tell three more things.

Telling the Story

- How did it happen?
- What led up to it happening?
- Why did you choose what you did?
- What were your alternatives?
- Why did you *not* choose something else?
- What did you expect to happen?
- What was the outcome?
- What did you learn from it?
- How did this change your life?

Emotional Integrity – Mad, Sad or Glad

- How did you feel about it at the beginning?
- How do you feel about it looking back on it?

Some Reflective Questions

The following are some open-ended questions to get the mental juices flowing. You may want to ponder these for a while before actually recording yourself or sitting at the keyboard.

- What have you read that has influenced your life the most?
- What person in your life was most influential in making you who you are?
- What experience in your life most shaped the person you are?
- What part has your religion had in shaping your life?
- What part did your life's work have on your life?
- What meaning has family life had for you?
- If you had to write your own epitaph, what would you say?
- What would you like to be remembered for?
- How would you describe your personality?
- How would you describe what you value most in life?
- What are the most important lessons you've learned in life?
- What has been your favorite saying?
- What's the nicest thing anyone ever said to you?
- What's the best thing you ever did for someone else?
- What are the most important things about how one should live a life?
- What was the biggest mistake you ever made?

Topics to Ask Yourself About

Consider adding a section somewhere in your text that reveals your thoughts and opinions of a variety of topics. This adds texture to your personality and an enticing zest to the story.

- Academics
- Bill of Rights
- Civil Rights
- Columnists
- Congress
- Cooking
- Fashion
- Fast Food
- Fine Dining
- Free Speech
- Fun
- Funerals
- Favorites:
  - Book(s)
  - Movie(s)
  - Play(s)
  - Author(s)
  - Song(s)
  - Music
- Artwork
- Geography
- Sites
- Gambling
- Gardening
- Great Art
- Great Men/Women
- Great Philosophers
- Great Presidents
- Great Truths
- Greatest Frustration
- Greatest Satisfaction
- Hobbies
- Learning
- Manual Labor
- Medicine
- Most Influential People in Your Life
- Parenting

Topics to Ask Yourself About

- Patriotism
- Personal Treasures
- Pet Peeves
- Pets
- Philosophy
- Public Education
- Religion
- Schools
- Science
- The Supernatural
- Spirits / Liquor
- Sports
- Taxes
- Teachers
- Technology
- The Future of Mankind
- The Golden Rule
- The Good Life
- The Good Person
- The Life Well Lived
- The Presidency
- Things You Always Say
- Things You're Most Pleased With
- U.S. Constitution
- U.S. Courts
- UFO's
- United Nations
- War
- Weddings
- Work
- Your Favorite Creations

The Whole You

"I always wanted to be somebody, but I should have been more specific."

-- Lily Tomlin

The idea behind this book you're writing is to let people know who you are or were as the case will be. I encourage you not to hold back. You are not too plain, but you could choose to be. You would be too humble if you choose to leave this life as anonymous as an ant. Any life told with sufficient detail and feeling is significant and interesting.

You needn't be gruesome or gratuitous in telling your story. But leave us more than the broth. Tell us who you were in full color, in meaningful detail. Add substance to your life's story by revealing the real you. Be somebody. Be specific.

About the Author:

David Eubanks is a personal historian who has recorded the oral histories of numerous individuals and published their stories in a book. David spent twenty-five years as a business communications specialist with experience in a variety of writing styles including procedure and policy manuals, training guides, websites, ad and packaging copy. He is the  creator of a technical writing course, *Word Mapping* ^{SM}. He has written one novel, *Double Cross*. He has worked as marriage and family counselor and has an M.A. in Family and Child Studies. Mr. Eubanks resides in Warrenville, Illinois where he works in his own firm writing personal biographies. He is a member of the Association of Personal Historians.

24W451 Emerald Green Warrenville, Illinois 60555
phone: 630-205-2546 e-mail: dveub@cs.com
www.david-eubanks.com

Made in the USA